HEARING T

HEARING THE CALL

Stories of young vocation

Jonathan Lawson and
Gordon Mursell

First published in Great Britain in 2014

Society for Promoting Christian Knowledge
36 Causton Street
London SW1P 4ST
www.spckpublishing.co.uk

British Library Cataloguing-in-Publication Data
A catalogue record for this book is available from the British Library

ISBN 978–0–281–07060–2
eBook ISBN 978–0–281–07061–9

eBook by Graphicraft Limited, Hong Kong

Typeset by Graphicraft Limited, Hong Kong
First printed in Great Britain by Ashford Colour Press
Subsequently digitally printed in Great Britain

Produced on paper from sustainable forests

Contents

Foreword by Rowan Williams   vii

Introduction   ix

1 Hearing the call (1 Samuel 3.1–20)
  How others can help with that. A call needs to be 'heard'   1

2 Understanding the call (Exodus 3.1–15)
  *God speaks in different ways from us; how do we
  know what he's saying?*   12

3 Surely it's not me? (Jeremiah 1.1–10)
  Am I up to doing this? People like me don't get ordained   22

4 The foolishness of God's call (Jonah 1)
  God's call often makes no sense at all   36

5 The counter-cultural nature of call (Ruth 1.16–18)
  *Being called means growing into the person God called you
  to be. That is necessarily about being different from others*   52

6 The subversive nature of God's call (Luke 1.26–38)
  *God calls us out of our comfort zone, and calls us to
  call others to that place too*   64

7 God's call and failure (Isaiah 6)
  *In a culture of success, driven by targets, we sometimes
  forget that some of the acclaimed leaders of the Church
  were, in practical terms at least, complete failures*   77

8 'Let anyone who has an ear listen to what the Spirit
  is saying to the churches' (Revelation 2.29)   93

  Endnote   103

Notes   116

AMDG
and in deep gratitude
to those who have shared their stories
of discerning God's will with us

Foreword

---•◆•---

Quite often when people say 'God has a purpose for your life', it's supposed to be reassuring. Second thoughts may suggest, though, that it's anything but. Most of us rebel at the idea that someone else has written a script we have to perform – and actually, if that's how we think of God's purposes, we're right to rebel. But the hard thing to grasp is that, because God has made us and invested the most costly kind of love in our lives, God understands more than we ever can or shall about what really makes us flourish, indeed, what makes us *real*. So his purpose is always, simply, to make us real, so that we may have the sort of joy nothing can take away. When he opens a door (or sometimes pushes you straight through one), it's his way of saying, 'You could be more than you realize, the world is bigger and stranger than you ever thought.'

A 'vocation' isn't some weird and unusual thing: it's just the way in which we (all of us) recognize all this. God wants to move us on towards reality, honesty and fullness of life; and from time to time, we get a deepened sense of how he's at work and where he's inviting us to discover this. It doesn't take long to realize that these invitations are likely to take us well beyond our comfort zones – just because we're all of us used to seeing less of ourselves than is really there. We sense, somehow, that we're being prodded into territory that is strange and not at all safe, even though we recognize at the same time that there's something about it that really matters to us and for us.

So no – 'reassuring' isn't the word. But talking about God's purpose and God's calling to us, about 'vocation', turns out to be something to do with growing in ways we couldn't have expected. One of the real strengths of this very good book is that it sets out lots of stories about how this sense of being invited into new territory can feel. It is very honest about the fact that people may react with anger or blind panic to such invitations; just as some react with a sense of 'so *that's* it', with joy and gratitude. Equally real and equally important responses: what matters is to let the response be truthful and then to take the next step in trust.

In the last few years, the Church of England has been underlining the importance of encouraging younger people to open up to God's invitation at a deeper level. Sometimes the Church in recent decades has been a bit uncertain about recognizing vocations to priesthood or other sorts of dedicated Christian life at a young age. But I think we've all been the losers from this; and we're beginning to do better.

In this book, you'll find a readiness to start from where you are, to take your experience of faith and trust seriously, and to offer some resources and a bit of a framework to make fuller sense of it. I hope and pray that, as you read, you'll catch some of the excitement there is in recognizing these moments of opening up and new possibility. This is the excitement of knowing that God may be prompting you to discover who you most truly are in and through serving the Christian family in ordained ministry or some other lifelong commitment of prayer and love. May the God who longs for our joy bring his Presence alive for you in these pages.

Rowan Williams
Magdalene College, Cambridge

Introduction

At the core of this book is an invitation to listen to what God is calling us to be. It is the authors' understanding that all human beings have a vocation and that it is no greater to be called to ordination than to serve God in any other way. However, although *Hearing the Call* is intended to benefit anyone hoping to discover God's will for them, it will be particularly helpful to young people trying to discern if they are called to be ordained – and the laity and clergy who will be involved in supporting, encouraging and nurturing them.

Each chapter of the book begins with a biblical story of someone being called by God. Jonathan Lawson, whose ministry at the University of Durham involves listening to and supporting those who are discerning their vocation, then reflects on his experience of discernment with young people in relation to the passage in question. In the 'Reflection' section that follows, Gordon Mursell explores what this biblical passage might mean in a broader context, drawing out its message for the world and for us today.

As such the book tries to mirror what it is about: learning how to listen to what God is calling us to be. How do we discern God's purpose for us? How do we hear his call? That's what we're about to explore.

1

Hearing the call

———◆•◆•◆———

Now the boy Samuel was ministering to the LORD under Eli. The word of the LORD was rare in those days; visions were not widespread.

At that time Eli, whose eyesight had begun to grow dim so that he could not see, was lying down in his room; the lamp of God had not yet gone out, and Samuel was lying down in the temple of the LORD, where the ark of God was. Then the LORD called, 'Samuel! Samuel!' and he said, 'Here I am!' and ran to Eli, and said, 'Here I am, for you called me.' But he said, 'I did not call; lie down again.' So he went and lay down. The LORD called again, 'Samuel!' Samuel got up and went to Eli, and said, 'Here I am, for you called me.' But he said, 'I did not call, my son; lie down again.' Now Samuel did not yet know the LORD, and the word of the LORD had not yet been revealed to him. The LORD called Samuel again, a third time. And he got up and went to Eli, and said, 'Here I am, for you called me.' Then Eli perceived that the LORD was calling the boy. Therefore Eli said to Samuel, 'Go, lie down; and if he calls you, you shall say, "Speak, LORD, for your servant is listening."' So Samuel went and lay down in his place.

Now the LORD came and stood there, calling as before, 'Samuel! Samuel!' And Samuel said, 'Speak, for your servant is listening.' Then the LORD said to Samuel, 'See, I am about to do something in Israel that will make both ears of anyone who hears of it tingle. On that day I will fulfil against Eli all that I have spoken concerning his house, from beginning

1

to end. For I have told him that I am about to punish his house for ever, for the iniquity that he knew, because his sons were blaspheming God, and he did not restrain them. Therefore I swear to the house of Eli that the iniquity of Eli's house shall not be expiated by sacrifice or offering for ever.'

Samuel lay there until morning; then he opened the doors of the house of the LORD. Samuel was afraid to tell the vision to Eli. But Eli called Samuel and said, 'Samuel, my son.' He said, 'Here I am.' Eli said, 'What was it that he told you? Do not hide it from me. May God do so to you and more also, if you hide anything from me of all that he told you.' So Samuel told him everything and hid nothing from him. Then he said, 'It is the LORD; let him do what seems good to him.'

As Samuel grew up, the LORD was with him and let none of his words fall to the ground. And all Israel from Dan to Beer-sheba knew that Samuel was a trustworthy prophet of the LORD.   (1 Samuel 3.1–20)

I, Jonathan, grew up in a prosperous part of south-east Surrey, and from early childhood went to church with my family. I starred in some nativity plays, was helped to project my voice by my Sunday school teacher who had trained at RADA (surely that can only happen in Surrey), sang in the church choir, learned to bellring as my father had done before me, and later became a server. At my preparatory school I had an enthusiastic religious education teacher who ran a Scripture Union group, which I attended; later I became a sacristan, looked after the chapel, and from my own motivation cleaned the brasses and rebound the hymn books.

Until recently I looked back on this part of my life with some embarrassment, wondering how I could have been so pious from such an early age. But more recently I have learned to honour and respect this part of my faith journey. I can see now with hindsight that God was stirring a sense of call in me to serve him. It is quite common to see only in retrospect what

God has been up to, but it might be worth reflecting on what has drawn you to read this book. Is God gently nudging you towards something? Do you feel that you might be meant to be more than you are now?

The realization that God had been guiding me towards ordination from childhood became more explicit for me through a conversation with a potential ordinand here at Durham. By talking about his early sense of vocation, he brought alive in me what God had been doing when I was young: something I hadn't really noticed so clearly before.

I think it is interesting to observe that with the call of Samuel, the nearly blind Eli helps the young, clear-sighted Samuel to see something he cannot see, while Samuel has the unenviable task of showing Eli something he has failed to grasp. Discernment is like a dance: both parties participate and both are changed by the exchange. It is, I believe, essential that anyone who is ministering in the work of discernment continues to strive towards understanding God's call for them personally. None of us has this all 'sorted', and the discernment of God's will for us is a lifelong journey.

But back to the Durham conversation. It became very clear that this individual had a call that had been waiting to be recognized for many years, and hearing his story seemed close to a mystical experience. As a boy, he had felt that he wished to serve God, and this feeling had become particularly intense at school. As he described longing to be close to Christ, our conversation had such a charge to it that I felt as though the door of his soul were open and I was glimpsing the glory of God. I can describe it in no other way. There was an incredibly strong sense that he needed someone to hear what he had been aware of for such a long time: a deep desire to love and serve God.

This experience led me to two profound reflections. First, that vocation is very often (though not always) there from an early age. I can recognize in my own unarticulated sense of call as a small boy an experience of being drawn to serve

God. Which is why I love the story of the call of Samuel: that boy serving God in the Temple powerfully echoes what I went through myself. My second reflection is on the importance of a call being heard. Now on one level this seems blindingly obvious. But as any good listener knows, we can sometimes only 'hear' things when they have been received by another – when they have been externalized, said out aloud. It is therefore a really important prerequisite if you are considering your sense of vocation that you talk to someone you trust, who will take seriously and handle sensitively what you tell them. Hearing someone talk about their sense of vocation, particularly for the first time, is like receiving a precious and fragile gift, one that deserves to be accepted with gratitude and respect.

For some individuals, there may be no thread of God's call through childhood to follow; rather, they experience a dramatic awakening. One member of our vocation group simply woke up one day when she was 17 and said to her father: 'I'm going to be a priest.' They talked about this with other members of the family, one of whom quite wisely suggested that she start going to church. So excitedly she went: she walked through the door of the church and said with great eagerness to a member of the congregation: 'I'm going to be a priest.'

'We don't believe in that here,' was the response. The Church of England has within its membership people with differing views on the ordination of women to the priesthood, but it is worth noticing the effect this had on the 17-year-old. She didn't speak about entering the priesthood again until she went to university.

Here is what another member of the Durham University Group, Peter Garvie, who is now a priest, has written about his own vocational journey:

The idea that God works within creation and within our lives was something that was completely foreign to me. I had had a good education, felt I had a moral compass, and would have perhaps even described myself as a Christian. That was it, I went off to university in Birmingham to study business studies and 'I' was in control. 'I' was deciding my own future. God put an end to that. And this is why the mystery of the individual vocation is so unfathomable to me; for myself, I didn't have my vocation immediately recognized by other Christians at church, God didn't physically or audibly appear to me and say, 'I want you to do this'. It is something far more subtle and difficult to understand, something that is still going on now, I believe for each of us. When I was 19 I opened up a Gideon Bible that was in my room at university and started reading the Psalms. Here I found psalms, some of which have been written by someone who has allowed themselves to be completely open and honest before God, and I wanted to do the same. An important moment for me was reading the beginning of the 37th Psalm: 'I will put my trust in the Lord, and he will give me my heart's desire.' At the time that certainly did not mean the ministerial priesthood, but it did mean coming to realize the reality of my own baptism and being guided by my own faith. I was confirmed and became a regular communicant, and the church became the place where I could pray, be loved and receive communion as I worked out 'with fear and trembling' my own vocation. This took me on an amazing journey: I left university in Birmingham and worked alongside young adults with severe learning disabilities, supporting them to live as independently as possible, I challenged myself, went travelling on my own, and read a lot of books. Eventually I was convinced to go back to university to study Theology, where I enjoyed a very formative three years at Durham. And my vocation to the priesthood began to be articulated in ways I could handle; for me it was more like an intuition, a gentle nagging that said, 'You need to find out more about this'. My college chaplain was very understanding and suggested ways of finding out more about whether this ministry was for me. I went to an inner-city church for Holy Week and found myself looking at other priests and saying to God, 'Is this realistically something I could do?' To help answer that question, and to get some more experience, I spent a year in

London working for a church in a challenging area, living in a community with three other people in a similar stage of discernment to me. The role included pastoral church work, especially working with some of the church's neediest people, often on the fringes, as well as coordinating a night shelter for the homeless. All this was valuable experience I continue to rely on today. It was during this time that with the help and support of my sending diocese I went to a diocesan selection conference and then to a Bishops' Advisory Panel, and so began my time at seminary, which was where the journey of real discernment began . . .

Taking anyone's sense of vocation seriously is of the utmost importance. For young people, such a sense is often on the cusp of consciousness, as are so many things when we are young. It takes grace to notice a call, and the moment of potentially bringing it to birth in words is both exciting and precarious. Imagine if Eli had told Samuel to go away and get some sleep? What if he had just not taken him seriously?

Yes, a call needs to be heard, and it often requires another to help with the hearing of it. Bringing anything out into the open for the first time is likely to involve fear of rejection, of not being understood or of not being accepted, so these first conversations are vital. If a negative response is perceived by someone experiencing God's call to ordained ministry, they may not speak about their vocation again for years. It can make all the difference between being ordained at twenty-something or much later in life. An old university friend said to me once that if there had been someone working with young vocations when she was at university, she might have been ordained a couple of decades earlier. It is also worth noting that the 'process' itself is part of the 'hearing' experience. It is a common complaint from candidates (particularly young candidates) to feel that they are not being heard or taken seriously, as they have had little or no contact with the person who is supporting them through the process. The 'unsaid' then becomes as important as the 'said'. I find that candidates often want to have at least a sense of the landscape of the discernment process, so that they can navigate it, and know that they are still being taken seriously. This book is in part trying to provide just that.

The discernment of young vocations and the encouragement of the discernment of young vocations is an important matter for the Church. For many years there was a culture whereby young adults who had a strong sense of call were sent away to get some 'life experience'. The Church of England has since come to realize the detrimental effect this has had on the numbers of young people coming forward for ordination, and although those numbers have now begun to increase, it seems that a change in culture within the Church is still required. I suspect we need to think about how we portray the life of a priest to young people (it being particularly important that they have good role models – not seemingly perfect priests, but priests who reflect that their vocation has brought them to life); to use the language of discernment more; and to develop greater sensitivity to the fact that God can and does call some people to ordained ministry from an early age. We should celebrate that fact. It is a good thing to have young priests! It is good to have older ones too!

During the school years, a sense of vocation may simply be something to observe, rejoice in and pray about. When someone reaches their late teens or early twenties, however, my experience tells me that it can be appropriate to ask: 'Have you thought about ordination?' In fact I believe it is really important to articulate that question sometimes. A student who was in our chapel choir so clearly had a sense of call to ordination that in his third week here as an undergraduate I asked him if he was going to be a priest: two years later he came back to discuss this with me. Recently he has been recommended for ordination training. He now says that, in retrospect, my asking if he had a vocation to ordained ministry was very important. It planted a seed. It opened up a vista – a horizon of possibility. Obviously this asking needs to be done with caution, thoughtfulness and prayer. I'm not suggesting asking every single person. However, as a naturally shy individual myself, I have learned that some precociousness is important when it comes to encouraging young vocations.

My favourite example of that precociousness was with a third-year undergraduate who went to choral evensong in Durham Cathedral almost every day. I took some soundings from the clergy at the Cathedral, and then one day I chatted to him and said: 'You come to evensong far too often. You're clearly going to be ordained. If you're going to be ordained you need to see me.' I gave him my card. A few weeks later he got in touch. Within a few months he was on placement in a set of parishes in London for a year, and now he is training to be ordained. Such precociousness is a risk and takes some courage, but it's often worth a try.

In Durham we, like other university chaplaincies, run a University Vocations Group. It is nothing grand. Often we just meet in the pub. Sometimes we have a speaker. Sometimes we watch a film. Sometimes we visit a particular project or parish. But my strong suspicion is that the most important work the group does is to meet. For in doing so, young people realize that other young people feel something similar to them. They are not alone. They are not crazy. Just knowing this helps them to take God's call more seriously. So if you can, find another young person who is thinking about ordination. If you cannot locate anyone locally, you might get in touch with your 'Young Vocations Champion' in the diocese, or use the 'Call Waiting' website to find out about young vocations events, where you'll meet lots of other young people thinking about ordination. They exist: you just need to find them!

In the vocations group here in Durham, we sometimes discuss the age people were when they felt called to ordination. One of the group remarked that she had been baptizing her teddy bears at the age of three! I am certainly not suggesting that children are bought Action Men to be dressed up as priests, nor that books are written on 'how to be a priest' aimed at the under-fives. But just as 'Godly play' tries to help children begin to learn how to handle sacred texts from an early age, so I think we could pay more attention in the Church to how we help young individuals discern God's will for them. This might be as simple as doing what Eli did for Samuel, and sending them back with a new understanding of how to listen to God.

Reflection

It's an extraordinary thought that God might be calling people, and opening up new possibilities for them, before they even know who or what God is. Faith will be essential if that call is to be accepted and followed, but it is not a prerequisite of being called. God has plans and hopes for the most fervent agnostics and sceptics, if only they knew it. At least this, in effect, is what the Bible tells us, and nowhere more graphically than in the story of the call of Samuel.[1]

The account, in the First Book of Samuel, took place while Samuel was still a boy (1 Sam. 3.1), and at a time when 'Samuel did not yet know the LORD' (3.7). Furthermore it happened at a time when 'the word of the LORD was rare . . . [and] visions were not widespread' (3.1). That time, in other words, was not auspicious for people of faith: the wind was against them. In the northern hemisphere at the start of the twenty-first century, it still is. Which only makes the story of Samuel's call the more relevant and surprising.

It takes place against a background of barrenness and despair. Hannah, Samuel's mother, is childless, and is taunted by her husband's other wife (1.6). In her bitterness, Hannah pours out her feelings before God in the Jerusalem Temple (1.11), and her prayer is answered: she conceives and gives birth. Overwhelmed with gratitude, she dedicates the child to God: the gift is not held on to or controlled, but offered back to the Giver. This is the exact opposite of a consumerist society: there is a sense in which God's initiative in calling Samuel is made possible by his parents' willingness to let go, not privatize or confine, the new life they receive. This is not neglect: Hannah loves her child (see 2.19). Rather, she wants this utterly unexpected and gracious gift to be released for its full potential to be realized, in response to God's call and purpose.

We are told that God calls Samuel when the boy was 'lying down' (3.3). God is at work in that confused yet fertile region of our interior lives where dream and vision, reality and fantasy, alertness and sleep interpenetrate one another. Unsurprisingly, and even though he is called by name, Samuel has no idea it is God who calls. So he goes to the priest, thinking it was he who called him (3.5).

And here the text becomes subversive, as all accounts of vocation in Scripture do in one way or another. Eli, the priest, is a mess: the public face of the national religious institution of the day, yet someone with a chaotic private life – he can't control his own sons (2.12). It was an institution in decline: in the state it was in, it had no future. And the person who will transform it radically is precisely the boy who here seeks guidance from the priest he will supplant, though neither of them knew it then. The young Samuel is in effect asking Eli: is my call from you? Eli could have said it was; or he could have told Samuel he was imagining things, and should go back to sleep. He did neither. He 'perceived that the LORD was calling the boy' (3.8), and told Samuel to listen to what God had to say. Even when (the next day) Eli hears the terrible commission that God offers to Samuel, a commission that involves the wholesale transformation of everything Eli had lived for and the ending of Eli's own life, Eli recognizes that God is at work: 'Then [Eli] said, "It is the LORD; let him do what seems good to him"' (3.18).

There is a profound sense in this story in which the old and the new need one another. The institution cannot continue as it is: God is 'about to do something in Israel that will make both ears of anyone who hears of it tingle' (3.11). Yet that does not mean that the ministry of Eli, the public religious figure with the private life in a mess, was in vain. He plays a modest but crucial pastoral role, both in gently affirming the distraught Hannah when she first pours out her sorrow before God, and then in recognizing that it was God who was calling Samuel, even though that call would draw a line under Eli's life. So Samuel needed Eli; but Eli needed Samuel, for without him Israel had no future at all. At some deep level, Eli is able to see that the larger purposes of God are greater than the narrow interests of a religious institution and his own personal hopes.

Here is the challenge of nurturing young vocations. We may well wonder how many vocations have gone unnoticed and unheard because those of us who inhabit the world of institutional faith have been unwilling to accept not only that God will call people utterly different from us, but also that those people's vocations may well be to transform completely the Church as we know it. Yet the story of Samuel's call suggests three things. First, it is precisely at a time of religious decline that God is calling young people, some of whom may well not even be sure whether they believe in God or not. Second, if they choose to respond to that call they will help God to do something that 'will make both ears of anyone who hears of it tingle'. Third, to the older, sometimes world-weary or disillusioned, representatives of the people of God, there is a twofold call. Such a call is no less vital, both to cradle and comfort the desperate and distraught, and to affirm and guide young people aware of some kind of spiritual impulse deep within but unsure of what it means – even at the cost of our own hopes and plans for the future. And to do this demands that same self-effacing and profound wisdom that Eli, the embodiment of priestly failure and disappointment, supremely made his own: 'It is the LORD; let him do what seems good to him.'

2

Understanding the call

Moses was keeping the flock of his father-in-law Jethro,
the priest of Midian; he led his flock beyond the wilder-
ness, and came to Horeb, the mountain of God. There the
angel of the LORD appeared to him in a flame of fire out
of a bush; he looked, and the bush was blazing, yet it was
not consumed. Then Moses said, 'I must turn aside and
look at this great sight, and see why the bush is not burned
up.' When the LORD saw that he had turned aside to see,
God called to him out of the bush, 'Moses, Moses!' And
he said, 'Here I am.' Then he said, 'Come no closer! Remove
the sandals from your feet, for the place on which you are
standing is holy ground.' He said further, 'I am the God
of your father, the God of Abraham, the God of Isaac, and
the God of Jacob.' And Moses hid his face, for he was afraid
to look at God.

Then the LORD said, 'I have observed the misery of my
people who are in Egypt; I have heard their cry on account
of their taskmasters. Indeed, I know their sufferings, and
I have come down to deliver them from the Egyptians,
and to bring them up out of that land to a good and broad
land, a land flowing with milk and honey, to the country
of the Canaanites, the Hittites, the Amorites, the Perizzites,
the Hivites, and the Jebusites. The cry of the Israelites
has now come to me; I have also seen how the Egyptians
oppress them. So come, I will send you to Pharaoh to
bring my people, the Israelites, out of Egypt.' But Moses
said to God, 'Who am I that I should go to Pharaoh, and

bring the Israelites out of Egypt?' He said, 'I will be with you; and this shall be the sign for you that it is I who sent you: when you have brought the people out of Egypt, you shall worship God on this mountain.'

But Moses said to God, 'If I come to the Israelites and say to them, "The God of your ancestors has sent me to you", and they ask me, "What is his name?" what shall I say to them?' God said to Moses, 'I AM WHO I AM.' He said further, 'Thus you shall say to the Israelites, "I AM has sent me to you."' God also said to Moses, 'Thus you shall say to the Israelites, "The LORD, the God of your ancestors, the God of Abraham, the God of Isaac, and the God of Jacob, has sent me to you":

> This is my name for ever,
> and this my title for all generations.'
>
> (Exodus 3.1–15)

One of the most common questions I am asked in my ministry as a vocation adviser, along with, 'Do you think I have a call to ordained ministry?', is: 'How do I know if I have a vocation to ordained ministry?' It's a very good question: after all, how do we ever know what God is calling us to be and do? But from my experience there are several tried and tested ways of getting a sense. The first, as we explored in the last chapter, is to begin to say it out aloud. The stirrings of God are generally internal, and at some point that needs to be articulated. Indeed, I suspect the whole discernment process is about trying to put that which is inexpressible and seemingly unutterable into words. The things of God are hard to describe. Sometimes it can be helpful to find a symbol or an image to describe what you're feeling. Many potential ordinands describe a sense of a gentle tug or a magnetic pull towards ordination. Some are aware of being unsettled, or of a persistent 'niggle', or of being led in a particular direction. Very recently an individual I was seeing gave me the image of her sense of call to ordination as like having a small stone in your shoe: it was fine most of the time, but at other times it became really annoying and irritating, and hard to ignore. Certainly, if you have a vocation to ordination it doesn't go away, and quite often others notice a sense of calling to ordination in us long before we do.

On some occasions I ask potential ordinands where they feel the sense of call in their bodies. One individual, who is now ordained and a friend, thought I was a bit odd when I asked him that some years ago, but that question can often reveal a lot. Many answer by pointing to their head or to their heart, although another mentioned his tongue, thinking of the call of Isaiah. Some say that they feel it all over their body, and for some the sense of call can feel very physical as well as spiritual.

However, it's important to note that thinking about vocation isn't the same as trying to hear what God is saying. One candidate I remember, who is now ordained, was particularly cerebral. Each of our meetings felt a bit like a theology oral exam, and this person was concerned to get the answers 'right'. In essence, he was unsure whether God was calling him to be a doctor or a priest. I act in these situations largely based on my intuition. So I asked him a question, one that I am not sure I have ever asked another candidate. I said: 'If you were to die tomorrow, which would you have preferred to have been: a priest or a doctor?' 'But I'm not going to die tomorrow,' he quickly retorted. 'But if you did?' I stubbornly replied. There was a long pause, and then he said: 'Priest'. Some years later, he told me that was a pivotal moment in discerning God's will for him.

There is one thing that I suggest to all those who come to see me who are thinking about ordination in order to help them sense if this is what God is calling them to be and do. That is to undertake a placement in a parish, when the time is right. Over the years, my experience is that this is a very effective way of seeing and experiencing if this feels right to the candidate, to those who meet him, and to those who are discerning whether that person has a vocation to ordination. I think this is effective for several reasons. One is that it plays to the gut instinct rather than to the head. All of us can have all sorts of ideas in our heads about ordained ministry, informed by many different things. A placement in a parish grounds our ideas and earths them. What a lot of clergy forget, of course, is that what a priest does all day looks particularly exciting to university students and to others of their generation, who see most of their peers going into careers and jobs that do not have the variety and freedom of parish ministry. The potential ordinand described above, who wasn't sure whether he was called to be a priest or a doctor, had travelled widely in the world, and yet he described his placement in a fairly standard parish in Sunderland as one of the most important experiences of his life at the time.

A placement in a parish also allows others to give feedback on whether those in the parish have seen the same sense of call as the potential ordinand and the person supporting him have seen. But I think the most important part of a placement is noticing the energy that comes from it, or doesn't come from it. For a religion that believes that God has come among us in human form in Jesus, we are not always very good at discovering God in our bodies. What brings us to life, and what doesn't, can give us hints of what God is calling us to be and do. A placement is often, from my experience, a very pivotal moment in the discernment process. There is this certain time I have noticed with young people, when sometimes they just suddenly get it. You can almost see it in their eyes – and it is usually combined with a great amount of energy, and a deep desire to do God's work. Although that energy and desire need to be tested, it is that energy that makes young vocations so exciting. It is not uncommon for that surge of energy and excitement to come after a placement.

On a practical level, a placement is usually something that I, as a vocation adviser, set up. It needs to be located somewhere that is attractive to a young person, but that doesn't mean it has to be a 'successful' place. Certainly, one potential ordinand who was sent from Durham to a buzzing church in another diocese asked if I might consider him for a second placement somewhere much rougher and more challenging, as he wanted something more gritty. The placement is usually for a week, staying either at the vicarage or rectory or in a parishioner's house. It is not meant to be something that costs the individual or the parish any significant amount of money. Often after a student has been at university we recommend that they undertake a year-long placement, but that is for very different reasons, and often the potential ordinand at that stage is quite some way along the path of discernment.

Reactions to going on a week's placement vary enormously, and can be everything from 'I want to be ordained tomorrow', to 'not on your life'. They tend to reveal a lot, as I say, not least from the feedback from the parish. This is particularly helpful to have, as most candidates for ordination are seen in one-to-one situations, which is quite correct considering the sensitivity of what is being discussed, but the disadvantage is that it is not possible to see how the candidate is with others. A placement also gives those who do not know the individual the opportunity to give a sense of how they found him. The placement is often something that is wonderfully mutually beneficial. It can give great hope to both parish priest and congregation to see God still calling young people to ministry. It can be very exciting for the young person to see the range of things a priest might do in a day, and the access a priest has to so many different parts of a community. Those on placement have been involved in a great range of activities, from preaching or leading the prayers in church to calling the bingo. For some it might be the first time they have encountered death and bereavement, or stood up in front of a class of children or a school assembly and told them a story. But most importantly it gives potential ordinands a strong and real sense of what ministry can be about. Quite a few of those I have seen over the years have been children of clergy. In my view it is particularly useful for them to do parish placements, as it is easy for them to think that they know what a parish priest does – and they do, from one perspective. However, it's very different when you're the one people are relating to as a potential future priest. It's important for them to get a sense of that.

But for some people a placement reveals either that this isn't the right thing, or more confusingly that it just isn't very clear. All of which is fine: a placement should never be set up as the only way truly to discover God's call; but it can be a 'sign', just as God gave Moses a sign both in the burning bush and when he states: 'this shall be the sign for you that it is I who sent you: when you have brought the people out of Egypt, you shall worship God on this mountain' (Exod. 3.12). Some potential ordinands explicitly ask God for a sign. One did just that, and not long afterwards a friend of his who was a strict atheist declared that she had been baptized at the Cathedral, largely because of his influence, and she told him that he should become a priest. As I said to him at the time, when it comes to signs, that seemed like quite a big one! But God often works in quieter and more discreet ways. It is worth noticing the reactions of friends and relatives if and when you tell them you are think-ing about this. What does your own church community think?

But sometimes we discover what we are called to do in life when we are doing something we don't like. A potential ordinand now training for ministry went on a placement a few years ago and really didn't enjoy it. I was flabbergasted. He had 'priest' practically tattooed to his forehead. He had served in church since the age of five. He went on placement with two other students, one of whom is now ordained and the other is in training. But it just didn't work for this guy, and when he graduated from Durham he got a secular job in London. He was good at what he did, but he hated it. Then he realized that his real desire was to be ordained. He undertook a year-long placement with a church group totally different from his own church tradition, and during that time was recommended for training. Of all the quotes I could give you from potential ordinands, his is my favourite. He says: 'Once God's got you, you're buggered.' It captures an important truth, because if God is calling you then there's no getting away from it! And running away, as we shall see in Jonah's story in Chapter 4, is a very common reaction to vocation.

But another guy on that same placement also has an interesting story. He did a year's placement after that in Durham Diocese, but for various reasons decided to train to be a teacher instead. Now, a few years later, he has been recommended for training. It is really important that candidates go at their own pace, and when they feel ready. At times I have to check my own enthusiasm to remind myself of that – it's vital that people aren't rushed. On the other hand, when they have got the bug and the energy then it's important that this is taken seriously and acted on. Young people don't often take 'going slow' very well, and there are plenty of other paths that they could follow.

Reflection

Moses is the least likely candidate to receive a vocation from God. He's part Hebrew, part Egyptian: Hebrew by birth, Egyptian by name and adoption (Exod. 2.2–10), and he grows up effectively belonging to neither (2.11–13); he's an ex-murderer (2.12), a refugee (2.15), married to the daughter of the priest of another faith (2.21), and an economic migrant (3.1). The message seems clear: if God can call Moses, God can call you or me.

Yet it isn't quite that simple. Moses is also a paradigm for God's new people. His very lack of clear nationality underlines the fact that when the people of Israel do leave Egypt, 'a mixed crowd also went up with them' (12.38). He will also have been bilingual, which allows him to address Pharaoh even though he is 'slow of speech' (4.10): the ability to speak different languages, and to enter into a culture different from your own, is a crucial gift for the priest or minister. And his willingness to learn from the wisdom that comes from other faiths (in Moses' case from his father-in-law, 18.1–27) without abandoning his own may have something to teach us too.

But there are far deeper senses in which the call of Moses may speak to us across the centuries. We may notice that Moses is *at work* when the call comes, 'keeping the flock of his father-in-law Jethro, the priest of Midian' (3.1); as with the shepherds on the night of Christmas, we may often be most receptive to God's call in places and at times when we least expect to be, and the workplace – the factory, the farm, the college library, the kitchen – may be the context for that call as often as the church or the retreat house. The call comes through the medium of a bush that is on fire yet not consumed, and Moses is drawn to it through sheer curiosity ('I must turn aside and look at this great sight', 3.3): only then does he hear God speaking to him (3.4). The presence of God in the midst of the everyday is object-ive (not merely a projection of Moses' experience or hopes), attractive (it draws yet does not compel), personal (God calls him by name) – but also life-changing. Note that Moses' initial 'Here I am' (3.4) becomes 'Who am I?' (3.11) once he's heard what God has in store for him: Christian vocation is never simply, or even primarily, the fulfilment of our psychological gifts or potential, but a radical unselfing that demands of us not just a complete change of life – one wonders what happened to Jethro's sheep – but also a complete rethinking of who we are.

And yet it is precisely at this moment, when Moses is pitched into urgent self-questioning, that God reveals the divine name to him: mysterious though that name is ('I AM WHO I AM', 3.14), it is the fullest self-manifestation by God before the incarnation of Jesus. And the God who reveals the divine name to Moses will come with him on his lonely journey to Pharaoh: 'I will be with your mouth and teach you what you are to speak' (4.12). Even when the conversation between God and Moses becomes fraught (Moses says at one point, 'O my Lord, please send some-one else', 4.13, which triggers God's anger), neither finally gives up on the other. And when Moses' eventual acceptance of his vocation leads to a profound sense of failure when Pharaoh takes no notice, he laments to God, 'Why did you ever send me? Since I first came to Pharaoh to speak in your name, he has mistreated this people, and you have done nothing at all to deliver your people' (5.22–23). Yet it is just this honest articulation of failure and bitter disappointment that leads to God assuring him of the ultimate fruitfulness of his vocation (6.1–8). Even then, Moses appears to achieve little: the Israelites 'would not listen to Moses, because of their broken spirit and their cruel slavery' (6.9). How are we to know whether our vocation is authentic, when even fellow Christians reject it? Only if it persists, and is finally life-changing for others as well as for us.

In the midst of such uncertainty, God offers Moses a sign that it really is God who is sending him: 'when you have brought the people out of Egypt, you shall worship God on this mountain' (3.12). The journey of the people of Israel, together with their fellow travellers, is not simply a journey from bondage to freedom but from bondage to *worship* – from helpless subjection to one kind of power to freely chosen worship of another. And, in the final analysis, this is what matters most: the heart of Moses' vocation (and of ours) is not about him (or us) at all – it's about God, and about the false powers that God confronts, and invites us to confront too. The story of the burning bush highlights in the most dramatic terms the difference between these two kinds of power and truth: the Pharaoh has no name (he is simply 'a new king . . . who did not know Joseph', 1.8), whereas the Lord reveals the divine name; the Pharaoh is reactive, where the Lord is proactive; the Pharaoh seeks to *control* people, where the Lord seeks to *change* them; the Pharaoh inspires fear, where the Lord inspires faith; the Pharaoh is a despot and a dictator, where the Lord is a nomad, travelling with the people in a pillar of cloud and fire (13.21–22).

And yet there is a final irony. The call of Moses will bear fruit beyond anything he could have imagined; but its fullest flowering will take place when he is no longer there to see it. In one of the most moving passages in the Bible, Moses climbs to the top of Mount Pisgah, where God shows him the promised land that his people will enter; but Moses doesn't live to go there with them – he dies while 'his sight was unimpaired and his vigour had not abated' (Deut. 34.7). Like Job, Moses is described as seeing God 'face to face' (Deut. 34.10; cf. Job 42.5); but he is told by the same God who had called him out of the burning bush that he won't see the fulfilment of that vocation:

> The LORD was angry with me because of you, and he vowed that I should not cross the Jordan and that I should not enter the good land that the LORD your God is giving for your possession. For I am going to die in this land without crossing over the Jordan, but you are going to cross over to take possession of that good land. So be careful not to forget the covenant . . .   (Deut. 4.21–23a)

To be called by God is no invitation to easy success or achievement. Others will reap what we sowed, just as we may reap what others have sowed before us. We may have to step aside and let others replace us just when we felt we were reaching our prime. If Moses had known all that lay in store for him, would he have accepted God's call from the burning bush, or would he have stayed with the sheep? The Bible doesn't answer that question because it isn't interested in it: instead, it describes Moses in the same way that a Trappist monk would one day describe his fellow monk Thomas Merton: 'He saw his whole life as a calling from God and one he was bound to answer faithfully. The calling did not make him: it was how he answered it that mattered. He tried to answer it with all he had.'[1]

3

Surely it's not me?

———•◆•———

The words of Jeremiah son of Hilkiah, of the priests who were in Anathoth in the land of Benjamin, to whom the word of the LORD came in the days of King Josiah son of Amon of Judah, in the thirteenth year of his reign. It came also in the days of King Jehoiakim son of Josiah of Judah, and until the end of the eleventh year of King Zedekiah son of Josiah of Judah, until the captivity of Jerusalem in the fifth month.

Now the word of the LORD came to me saying,

'Before I formed you in the womb I knew you,
and before you were born I consecrated you;
I appointed you a prophet to the nations.'

Then I said, 'Ah, Lord GOD! Truly I do not know how to speak, for I am only a boy.' But the LORD said to me,

'Do not say, "I am only a boy";
for you shall go to all to whom I send you,
and you shall speak whatever I command you.
Do not be afraid of them,
for I am with you to deliver you, says the LORD.'

Then the LORD put out his hand and touched my mouth; and the LORD said to me,

'Now I have put my words in your mouth.
See, today I appoint you over nations and over kingdoms,
to pluck up and to pull down,
to destroy and to overthrow,
to build and to plant.'

(Jeremiah 1.1–10)

The story of the call of Moses in the last chapter immediately reminds me of two things. The first is one potential ordinand who saw Moses as his role model, because of his own stutter. Moses, it states later in Exodus 4, 'is slow of speech' (4.10), and yet God calls him. This person had a stutter, but he learned to help himself through teaching himself to sing. He has the most beautiful tenor voice, and so what seemed like an impediment became a gift, not just to him but also to those who hear him sing. I commonly ask potential ordinands if they have a role model for their sense of call, from either the present or the past, and this particular individual mentioned Moses. But it wasn't just because of the stutter, I suspect, that he mentioned him. This man also had quite a colourful personal life, and another question I regularly ask potential ordinands is: 'What does God think of you?' This person's immediate answer was 'little shit'. I am often amazed at how few say, in answer to my question, that God loves them. Moses, as Gordon pointed out, also had an eventful past, and yet God still calls and chooses him: something that might well have an echo for many of us, as none of us have had perfect lives.

The second reminder is the 'standing [on] holy ground' (Exod. 3.5). Whenever individuals or members of a group open their souls to others, my experience is that that is holy ground. So those who are listeners and those who speak of such things need to be respectful of this and bow low to God's presence in that moment. This is particularly important with young candidates, and I have an image of vocation in young people as like that of a candle flame in the wind, easily buffeted about and also easily snuffed out. It can be as fragile as the tiny baby in the womb, referred to in the extract that heads this chapter.

This well-known passage from Jeremiah has echoes for me of John 15.16: 'You did not choose me but I chose you.' The sense of being chosen even before we were born is a very powerful one. But I think for many it captures something of the compulsion that a sense of vocation can have. To quote Parker Palmer: 'Vocation does not come from a voice "out there" calling me to be something I am not. It comes from a voice "in here" calling me to be the person I was born to be, to fulfil the original selfhood given me at birth by God.' He goes on to say: 'Vocation at its deepest level is, "This is something I can't not do, for reasons I am unable to explain to anyone else and don't fully understand myself but that are nonetheless compelling."'[1] Hence, once God's got you, you're buggered! (see p. 18).

My experience tells me that a sense of calling, be it to ordained ministry or to whatever God has called you to be and do, is insistent and does not go way. One example of this comes from a member of the Vocation Group in Durham who is now ordained. This is what she says about God's insistent call:

> So I began to be not ashamed in admitting to people I was a Christian. I still remained, and continue to this day, critical of some of the Church's theology and practices. But, I thought, rather than ignoring it I could engage with it and explore even deeper the infinite beauty and wonder that is God.
>
> But that is not to say that I was at all thinking about ordination, that was definitely not on my agenda. Having given up my ambitions of being Kylie's backing dancer or the British equivalent to Lenin, I settled on becoming an academic psychologist, and this career path was going well. Doing my own research in an area that fascinated me and teaching others about this passion of mine was something that I really loved. So I have to say, it wasn't exactly welcomed when I felt called once more to the priesthood. It happened one New Year's Day, when unbelievably hung over and believing my head was being bashed repeatedly by a boulder, my parents, who I was visiting, thought it would be nice if we visited Durham Cathedral. It was there, while standing at the back, looking down the nave towards the High Altar, I felt as if someone was gently – which was very kind considering my delicate state – but insistently whispering to me, 'Oh come on, I've called you to serve as a priest, how long will you keep saying no.' It was standing at the back that I threw in the towel and said, 'Okay, okay I'll think about it.'

However, I was convinced I hadn't got this right, maybe I was just being mad, so for a long time I kept this quiet. I believed, and still do, that I am not the sort of person who should be a priest. I speak before I think, I am extremely liberal in my views, I drink, swear, and am very, very irreverent. But one afternoon, a few years later, when me and my work colleagues had bunked off work to go to the pub, we started to talk about: if we didn't do our current job, what else would we do? When it came to my turn I said, 'I think I would be a priest.' Their response was anything but what I'd expected. I thought they would find it hilarious, me a priest, no way: I was the one who regularly argued aggressively with anyone who expressed a political view that I remotely disagreed with, who was forever crying over the latest heartbreak; I was the girl whose hair they had to hold back after indulging a little too much during a wild night clubbing. I thought, and hoped, they would tell me that the last thing I should ever do was become a priest. However, their response shocked me, for none of them was the least bit surprised and in fact they all had expected it, wondering why I even doubted it. In fact, as I told more friends and family, all of them gave a similar response, and in return a growing niggling sense that I really should do something serious about having this vocation became increasingly annoying.

Later in the book we shall look at running away from that sense of call. I remember a very experienced priest who had been a Diocesan Director of Ordinands talking about people in the parish who were hard to handle: in his experience this often came down to a thwarted vocation. Particularly, when the frustration is directed towards the Vicar, it's worth reflecting on whether it's because they really desire to be the Vicar themselves. In my own pastoral experience it rings true that at the heart of someone's self-destructive or disruptive behaviour there is often deep down a vulnerable, fragile part of them waiting to be heard, to be loved and to be healed. The challenge is learning how to do that. But the journey of discernment will always challenge us to love the unlovely parts of our lives as well as the less than attractive parts of the lives of others.

As far as I can understand, it is God's desire for us to fulfil the potential he has given us: to become who he made us to be. Very often that is about being in the places and environments where we can flourish. Again we are back to energy and growth, but also to a new theme of authenticity. What is it to be me? The 'I am who I am' of the burning bush. What is it to be myself?

Thomas Merton put all this very succinctly in his book *Seeds of Contemplation*. Early in the book he writes: 'For me to be a saint means to be myself.'[2] We are called to be who God made us to be. But he also points out the dangers, later in the book, when we don't allow that to happen, when we thwart our vocation:

> Souls are like wax waiting for a seal. By themselves they have no special identity. Their destiny is to be softened and prepared in this life, by God's will, to receive, at their death, the seal of their own degree of likeness to God in Christ.
>
> And this is what it means, among other things, to be judged by Christ.
>
> The wax that has melted in God's will can easily receive the stamp of an identity, the truth of what it was meant to be. But the wax that is hard and dry and brittle and without love will not take the seal: for the hard seal, descending upon it, grinds it to powder.
>
> Therefore if you spend your life trying to escape from the heat of the fire that is meant to soften and prepare you to become your true self, and if you try to keep your substance from melting in the fire – as if your true identity were to be hard wax – the seal will fall upon you at last and crush you. You will not be able to take your own true name and countenance, and you will be destroyed by the event that was meant to be your fulfilment.[3]

However, whether an individual grows more into what God made her to be is not just about her: it is also about the communities and people they relate to, including the Church. In a later chapter we shall look at what that might mean and the pressures that stop us being ourselves, which are immense. But the Church itself needs to be awake and aware of this, particularly in the way it relates to difference. Helping others to discern their sense of call therefore involves an openness to the other, to being surprised, to novelty.

Very often vocation and discipleship are seen to be about what I can do, rather than what I might become. That, I suspect, is at the heart of something I have heard many times from potential ordinands: 'I'm not sure I'm up to doing it' – being a priest, that is. It is something that most potential candidates have said to me at some point or other in the discernment process. That's quite a surprising thing to hear from students at a top British university, who are very capable young people. At one level it is a quite understandable reaction to an ever clearer sense that God might be calling you to ordained ministry. You might be feeling that as you read this now. How could *I* possibly do this? To be honest, I would be very worried by anyone who thought that they could, and Jeremiah is only one among many in the Bible whose instant reaction to being called is, in effect, 'I cannot do it.' 'How can I?' 'I am only a child.' But none of us can do it – that's the point. Only in God can we do anything.

An exercise often recommended when reading this story from Jeremiah is to insert your own name into the passage and listen to what God says to you, not just to Jeremiah. It's a way of hearing God's personal commission to us.

Some potential ordinands I have met have had lives in the past that might surprise many, if they knew about them in detail, considering they are contemplating ordination. Some never went to church as a child; others have done things they thought they shouldn't have done. One asked me if it was all right for an ordained person to have piercings and tattoos. In a world where the seemingly perfect is pushed in our faces through the media and advertising at a relentless rate, it is very easy to assume that we are called to be seemingly perfect priests as well. But I'm writing this on the Feast of the Conversion of St Paul, a reminder to us all that God can take those who persecute and kill believers, and transform their lives. God has always done this – taken the most unlikely people and used them for good. The Bible makes that clear. I love this poem, 'Getting it across', by U. A. Fanthorpe, who puts this in her own inimitable way:

'His disciples said unto him, Lo, now speakest thou plainly, and speakest no proverb. Now are we sure that thou knowest all things.'   (St. John 16: 29–30)

This is the hard thing.
Not being God, the Son of Man,
– I was born for that part –
But patiently incising on these yokel faces,
Mystified, bored and mortal,
The vital mnemonics they never remember.

There is enough of Man in my God
For me to construe their frowns. I feel
The jaw-cracking yawns they try to hide
When out I come with one of my old
Chestnuts. Christ! Not that bloody
Sower again, they are saying, or God!
Not the Prodigal bleeding Son.
Give us a new one, for Messiah's sake.

They know my unknowable parables as well
As each other's shaggy dog stories.
I say! I say! I say! There was this Samaritan,
This Philistine and this Roman . . . or
What did the high priest say
To the belly dancer? All they need
Is the cue for laughs. My sheep and goats,
Virgins, pigs, figtrees, loaves and lepers
Confuse them. Fishing, whether for fish or men,
Has unfitted them for analogy.

Yet these are my mouths. Through them only
Can I speak with Augustine, Aquinas, Martin, Paul
Regius Professors of Divinity,
And you, and you.
How can I cram the sense of Heaven's kingdom
Into our pidgin-Aramaic quayside jargon?

I envy Moses, who could choose
The diuturnity of stone for waymarks
Between man and Me. He broke the tablets,
Of course. I too know the easy messages
Are the ones not worth transmitting;
But he could at least carve.
The prophets too, however luckless
Their lives and instructions, inscribed on wood,
Papyrus, walls, their jaundiced oracles.

I alone must write on flesh. Not even
The congenial face of my Baptist cousin,
My crooked affinity Judas, who understands,
Men who would give me accurately to the unborn
As if I were something simple, like bread.
But Pete, with his headband stuffed with fishhooks,
His gift for rushing in where angels wouldn't,
Tom, for whom metaphor is anathema,
And James and John, who want the room at the top –
These numskulls are my medium. I called them.

I am tattooing God on their makeshift lives.
My Keystone Cops of disciples, always
Running absurdly away, or lying ineptly,
Cutting off ears and falling into the water,
These Sancho Panzas must tread my Quixote life,
Dying ridiculous and undignified,
Flayed and stoned and crucified upside down.
They are the dear, the human, the dense, for whom

My message is. That might, had I not touched them,
Have died decent respectable upright deaths in bed.[4]

As time has gone on in my ministry I have come to realize that
that sense of inadequacy can be a gift and a grace rather than
a curse. When we recognize that we cannot do something, then
God gets a look-in. We realize that he can do things perfectly
well without us. The world and the Church do not rely on us.
On my office wall I have a quote from Thomas Merton that
reminds me: 'Keep still, and let Him do some work.'[5] This is
God's work: the privilege is that he asks us to join him in doing
it. Then the sense of inadequacy can be transformed, as we learn
to refocus on God rather than ourselves: just as the ordinand
with the stutter has been transformed by learning to sing. The
impediment becomes a gift. We start to look at what God is
doing both in our lives and in the lives of others and to celebrate
that. It becomes less and less about us, and more and more about
God. Then it may be possible for us to see if we can create the
right environment for those things to continue and grow.

You could have a go at this now, while you're reading this book.
Notice what God is drawing you to. Give thanks for that, and
ask God as a friend for the grace to continue to reveal his will
for you. You could also try the Jesuit practice of the *examen*,
creating a time before God simply to notice where God has
been in your day: ask for the grace to notice the patterns – when
he seems more present and less present. Then say 'sorry' and 'thank
you' for what appears appropriate and ask for the graces that you
need for the next day. A book I have found helpful in this is
Sleeping with Bread.[6] It looks like a children's book, but it isn't!

In the nurture and formation of young vocations, we have
already begun to see that the sense of call, as with the call of
Jeremiah, can begin before we are even conscious of it; God
gives us the possibility of either accepting that call or rejecting
it, and he gives us that choice again and again. But the nurture
of that call has some urgency to it, in that acceptance brings

us to fuller life, and rejection to a diminished life. That is why the *examen* can be so useful, because it can help us to recognize what brings us to life and what diminishes our life. We begin to see a pattern: to discern the call for ourselves through God working within us. This can come, too, through the help of others who also bring us to life: not just through our own physical birth, but through a continual rebirth – and it is in the help of others, their example and encouragement, that we can become more fully the person God made us to be.

Just last summer, Biddy Baxter, who produced and then edited for 26 years the BBC children's programme *Blue Peter*, received an honorary degree from the University of Durham. In the oration at her graduation, given by Professor Simon Hackett, a story was quoted from her book that I found very moving:

In 2008, Biddy published a collection of some of the best letters from 50 years of the programme. They are a remarkable reflection of the changing nature of children's lives over the latter part of the twentieth century. Some are also very funny. Here is an extract from my favourite, written by Anthony, aged 9:

'This may seem strange but I think I know how to make people or animals alive. Why I'm teling you is because I can't get the things I need. A list of what I need:

Diagram of how everything works inside your body
Model of a heart split in half (both halves)
Tools for cutting people open
Tools for stitches
Fibreglass box, 8 foot tall, 3 foot width . . .'

Instead of dismissing this as nonsense, Biddy responded by encouraging Anthony to seek information for his idea from his family doctor. Anthony, now Professor of Rheumatology and Tissue Engineering at Bristol University, went on to pioneer the use of stem-cell technology in the treatment of arthritis. He believes that the whisper of encouragement that he gleaned from Biddy's reply was 'fundamental' to his future. *Blue Peter*, and Biddy Baxter, changed children's lives.[7]

I love that, and I particularly love that phrase, 'whisper of encouragement'. All of us, especially when we are young, need that 'whisper of encouragement' to gain confidence that we can be what we feel called to be. In the ministry of discernment, that encouragement is essential.

Reflection

In the story of Jeremiah's call, there appear to be only two characters: Jeremiah and the Lord. No intermediaries, not even a burning bush. But appearances are deceptive: there are other people involved, even though not all of them are explicitly mentioned.

The first of these is Jeremiah's mother. We know his father's name (Hilkiah, Jer. 1.1), but not his mother's; yet although she herself doesn't get a mention, her womb does – and not once but twice, in the Hebrew original. The King James Version is the closest to it:

> Then the word of the LORD came unto me, saying, Before I formed thee in the belly I knew thee; and before thou camest forth out of the womb I sanctified thee, and I ordained thee a prophet unto the nations.
>
> (Jer. 1.4–5, KJV)

Four active verbs, with God as the subject ('formed . . . knew . . . sanctified . . . ordained'), surround the unborn child as he lies in his mother's womb: the divine purpose is cradling little Jeremiah before he's even been born. Was his mother aware of this? It seems unlikely. But then we might ask ourselves: what new life might we be carrying that God's procreative and purposive word is calling into being? Not all of us are mothers; but all of us have the potential to bring to birth that new life, even though (as with Jeremiah's mother) that life may well not be intended only, or even primarily, for us. Yet her part is crucial too: the upbringing Jeremiah received, the dispositions he inherited, will have helped to shape his response to the divine call. The gifts God gives us, the new life that God forms deep within us, need our birthing and nurturing love if they are to fulfil God's purposes; and we may be amazed at what God can help us give birth to, if only we can believe it is there.

And there are other characters standing in the background of the story of Jeremiah's call. All of them are kings: Josiah son of Amon, Jehoiakim and Zedekiah sons of Josiah (1.1–3). These are genuine historical figures, who reigned in Jerusalem from 626 to 587 BCE. But their rule was terminated abruptly, as we are told: 'the captivity of Jerusalem in the fifth month' refers to the taking of the city and the deposition of the monarch by the Babylonian king Nebuchadnezzar. Jeremiah was born into a period of political upheaval, and his vocation will be irreducibly political. But not narrowly nationalist: note that he is to be a prophet 'to the nations' (1.5), not just to the people of Israel and Judah. We may note also that he is to be appointed 'over nations and over kingdoms' (1.10): a remarkable vocation for a country priest's son from a place called Anathoth (1.1). Yet that is just the point: in Scripture, the call of God frequently subverts established structures (as with Samuel and Moses), and here as elsewhere the young person who is called is told not to be afraid of those to whom he or she is sent (1.8).

It's not surprising that the young Jeremiah is gripped by a sense of personal inadequacy ('Ah, Lord GOD! Truly I do not know how to speak, for I am only a boy' 1.6), even though such a sense is common to many accounts of vocation. But in addition to the personal reassurance that he receives from God, the story of Jeremiah's call suggests that two other resources will help him accomplish the daunting challenge ahead of him. The first of these is words, the second imagination.

The story of Jeremiah's call, and the book that now bears his name, open with an explicit reference to words: 'The words of Jeremiah son of Hilkiah.' Words dominate the story of his call: intimate words ('Before I formed you in the womb I knew you'), children's words ('Ah, Lord GOD! Truly I do not know how to speak, for I am only a boy'), words of both destructive and creative power ('to pluck up and to pull down, to destroy and to overthrow, to build and to plant'). Most of the words are God's, not Jeremiah's; and this is crucial. If the prophet is truly to speak on behalf of God, he or she must first be able, as the Book of Common Prayer puts it, 'to hear *and receive* God's holy word'. The Bible is acutely aware of the dangers involved in substituting our words for God's:

> May the LORD cut off all flattering lips,
> the tongue that makes great boasts,
> those who say, 'With our tongues we will prevail;
> our lips are our own – who is our master?'
>
> (Ps. 12.3–4)

We live in a society saturated with words, many worthless and some deeply hurtful, but others capable of calling new life into being. It's worth our asking ourselves: what words will I choose to speak today? What words did I regret using? What words did God speak to me today, either directly or through an intermediary? Christian faith is centred upon the belief that, from all eternity, God spoke forth the living Word that had been with God since the beginning, a Word that became flesh and dwelt among us. Hence, as St Augustine says, 'the life of the speaker has greater weight in determining whether he or she is obediently heard than any grandness of eloquence.'[8]

'Then the LORD put out his hand and touched my mouth; and the LORD said to me, "Now I have put my words in your mouth"' (1.9). In speaking forth the words that God entrusts to him, in bringing to birth the truth that God has conceived within him, Jeremiah himself becomes a living word: his life becomes an embodiment of what he is called upon to speak. He is to be set apart, 'consecrated' or 'sanctified' (1.5), so that he can be a hearer and receiver of the divine word. Michelangelo's famous depiction of Jeremiah on the ceiling of the Sistine Chapel in Rome shows him seated, silent, deep in thought. Christian vocation will never simply be a call to *do* things: it will always first be a call to listen, and a call to be – to live in a particular way, so that your life is both conformed to, and authenticates, the words God wants you to speak. And when that happens, the powerful will be challenged, and the world will believe.

Yet for that to happen, we need more than just words: we also need imagination. For Jeremiah to respond at all to God's call involved a remarkable act of imagination on his part: he had to imagine God forming and shaping him in his mother's womb, and he had to imagine, and in some sense envisage, God's new future – of plucking up and pulling down, destroying and overthrowing, building and planting – coming into being. No one has written more eloquently about the power of the prophetic imagination than Walter Brueggemann, who has this to say about its role in the life of Jeremiah:

> Through poetic imagination, faithful listeners are invited to break with the make-believe world fostered by royal interest and join the poet's world. The poem fights for the imagination of Israel, to wean Israel away from excessive fascination with the visible power in Jerusalem.[9]

Here is the heart of the prophetic vocation: the powerless Jeremiah will be more powerful than the secular rulers of his day because he will out-imagine them; in the words he speaks, and the life he lives, the vision of God's new future will be brought to birth in and through him. It will be costly: his is perhaps the loneliest journey of all the biblical characters explored in this book, and challenging secular authority rarely makes for popularity. But he will help his people, and countless others who have come after him, to dream into being nothing less than a cosmos made new.

4

The foolishness of God's call

Now the word of the LORD came to Jonah son of Amittai, saying, 'Go at once to Nineveh, that great city, and cry out against it; for their wickedness has come up before me.' But Jonah set out to flee to Tarshish from the presence of the LORD. He went down to Joppa and found a ship going to Tarshish; so he paid his fare and went on board, to go with them to Tarshish, away from the presence of the LORD.

But the LORD hurled a great wind upon the sea, and such a mighty storm came upon the sea that the ship threatened to break up. Then the mariners were afraid, and each cried to his god. They threw the cargo that was in the ship into the sea, to lighten it for them. Jonah, meanwhile, had gone down into the hold of the ship and had lain down, and was fast asleep. The captain came and said to him, 'What are you doing sound asleep? Get up, call on your god! Perhaps the god will spare us a thought so that we do not perish.'

The sailors said to one another, 'Come, let us cast lots, so that we may know on whose account this calamity has come upon us.' So they cast lots, and the lot fell on Jonah. Then they said to him, 'Tell us why this calamity has come upon us. What is your occupation? Where do you come from? What is your country? And of what people are you?' 'I am a Hebrew,' he replied. 'I worship the LORD, the God of heaven, who made the sea and the dry land.' Then the men were even more afraid, and said to him, 'What is this that you have done!' For the men knew that he was fleeing from the presence of the LORD, because he had told them so.

Then they said to him, 'What shall we do to you, that the sea may quieten down for us?' For the sea was growing more and more tempestuous. He said to them, 'Pick me up and throw me into the sea; then the sea will quieten down for you; for I know it is because of me that this great storm has come upon you.' Nevertheless, the men rowed hard to bring the ship back to land, but they could not, for the sea grew more and more stormy against them. Then they cried out to the LORD, 'Please, O LORD, we pray, do not let us perish on account of this man's life. Do not make us guilty of innocent blood; for you, O LORD, have done as it pleased you.' So they picked Jonah up and threw him into the sea; and the sea ceased from its raging. Then the men feared the LORD even more, and they offered a sacrifice to the LORD and made vows.

But the LORD provided a large fish to swallow up Jonah; and Jonah was in the belly of the fish for three days and three nights.   (Jonah 1)

The tale of Jonah is one of my favourite vocation stories in the Bible, partly because it is very human and partly because it is so incredibly melodramatic. It also reminds me of how egotistical I am so often in my own ministry, forgetting, like Jonah, that what I have been asked to do is God's work, not mine, and for his glory, not mine.

The whole structure of the story itself is a parable of how many individuals experience a sense of God's call: Jonah is called by God. Jonah's first response is to run away. Jonah next gets on a boat and is thrown around in a storm (it is interesting to note that the storm could be interpreted as being caused by his not accepting his call from God, thus creating havoc for others). He jumps ship and enters the darkness of the belly of a large fish. Jonah is then 'spewed out' of the fish. He is called again by God, and this time he obeys. As a result of Jonah's actions Nineveh repents, and Jonah is mightily angry: now he looks a fool, as God hasn't done what he said he would and destroy Nineveh – rather, he has turned out to be a merciful God after all. Jonah sulks and wishes he were dead. God meets his anger with love and tenderness, demonstrating his power to bring life and to take it away again with the shelter he provides Jonah overnight.

I'm guessing that most human beings faced with something as dramatic as a sense of God's call are at some point going to want to run away from it. God's call is an awesome thing, and there is a lot to be frightened about. As I write this, the Church commemorates Maximilian Kolbe, a Franciscan priest who gave his life in the concentration camps of Auschwitz so that another might live. The call of God is often costly. There is much to be sacrificed: not only a potentially lucrative career, but also the sense of being in charge of your own life, and sometimes life itself. For a lot of students, part of their unease about going forward for ordination is the fear of the unknown.

I find the idea of the costly call to discipleship beautifully and humorously captured by Adrian Plass in this poem:

> When I became a Christian I said, Lord, now fill
>   me in,
> Tell me what I'll suffer in this world of shame and sin.
> He said, Your body may be killed, and left to rot
>   and stink,
> Do you still want to follow me? I said, Amen – I
>   think.
> I think Amen, Amen I think, I think I say Amen,
> I'm not completely sure, can you just run through
>   that again?
> You say my body may be killed and left to rot and
>   stink,
> Well, yes, that sounds terrific, Lord, I say Amen – I
>   think.

But, Lord, there must be other ways to follow you,
   I said,
I really would prefer to end up dying in my bed.
Well, yes, he said, you could put up with the sneers
   and scorn and spit,
Do you still want to follow me? I said Amen! – a bit.
A bit Amen, Amen a bit, a bit I say Amen,
I'm not entirely sure, can we just run through that
   again?
You say I could put up with sneers and also scorn
   and spit,
Well, yes, I've made my mind up, and I say, Amen! –
   a bit.

Well I sat back and thought a while, then tried a
   different ploy,
Now, Lord, I said, the Good Book says that
   Christians live in joy.
That's true he said, you need the joy to bear the
   pain and sorrow,
So do you want to follow me? I said, Amen! –
   tomorrow.
Tomorrow, Lord, I'll say it then, that's when I'll
   say Amen,
I need to get it clear, can I just run through that
   again?
You say that I will need the joy, to bear the pain
   and sorrow,
Well, yes, I think I've got it straight, I'll say Amen! –
   tomorrow.

He said, Look, I'm not asking you to spend an
   hour with me,
A quick salvation sandwich and a cup of sanctity,
The cost is you, not half of you, but every single bit,
Now tell me, will you follow me? I said Amen! – I quit.

39

I'm very sorry, Lord, I said, I'd like to follow you,
But I don't think religion is a manly thing to do.
He said, Forget religion then, and think about my Son,
And tell me if you're man enough to do what he
    has done.

Are you man enough to see the need, and man
    enough to go,
Man enough to care for those whom no one wants
    to know,
Man enough to say the thing that people hate to hear,
To battle through Gethsemane in loneliness and fear.
And listen! Are you man enough to stand it at the
    end,
The moment of betrayal by the kisses of a friend,
Are you man enough to hold your tongue, and
    man enough to cry,
When nails break your body – are you man enough
    to die?
Man enough to take the pain, and wear it like a crown,
Man enough to love the world and turn it upside
    down,
Are you man enough to follow me, I ask you once
    again?
I said, Oh, Lord, I'm frightened, but I also said Amen.
Amen, Amen, Amen, Amen; Amen, Amen, Amen,
I said, O Lord, I'm frightened, but I also said,
    Amen.[1]

It is a very common reaction to a suspicion of God's call to be afraid, maybe even terrified. The Bible is littered with stories of people being called, and their first reaction is fear. If you think about it, what else would you expect? And most of us run away when we are afraid. This is beautifully captured in the 2010 film *Of Gods and Men*: the true story of the Trappist monks in Algeria who had to make the hard decision about whether to leave the place they were committed to and be safe, or stay and potentially face death. They don't find an easy answer, but they do discover one that they become reconciled to over time, when they discern God's will for them. It is a hard film to watch, and yet brilliant in its depiction of both vocation and the grace that God gives us to discern his will: for ultimately, God does not often call us to be 'safe' – but what he has promised is that he will always be with us.

This is summed up for me by John Macmurray:

> The maxim of illusory religion runs: 'Fear not; trust in God and he will see that none of the things you fear will happen to you'; that of real religion, on the contrary, is: 'Fear not, the things that you are afraid of are quite likely to happen to you, but they are nothing to be afraid of.'[2]

Many candidates for ordination, especially those who are older, often talk about having run away from their sense of God's call all their lives, and about their sense of freedom in being able to stop running! One individual described a strong sense of feeling very unsettled, being upset enough to cry most days and not really understanding what was going on, until it suddenly came to her that she too might be called to be ordained. Then she gained a sense of peace and of purpose and clarity.

Here is what another wrote when she had a second sense of the same call in her life:

> When I was aged 14, at the height of my supposedly religious zeal, I went on pilgrimage to Walsingham, Norfolk. While there, praying alone in the Shrine of our Lady of Walsingham, I once again felt a profound and terrifying sense emerging deep within my body of being called by God to ordained ministry. This unasked and unwanted vocation appalled me, to the point that it caused me to stand up from what I suddenly regarded to be a demeaning position of kneeling and, angrily, storm out of the shrine.

When we feel like running, both physically and spiritually, there is often something to be said for doing the opposite: staying still until the fear subsides, or at least running towards somewhere safe. In my experience, decisions made in fear rarely turn out to be good ones; those that come from a sense of peace tend to be better ones.

But what follows with Jonah is also common to many people's experiences of discerning their vocation under God: they feel all at sea, bounced around and buffeted by waves, odd currents and the power of the wind. Vocation is very often disorienting. What is this that I can feel? Why is it so intangible? Is it true? What does this mean for who I am? Discerning God's call is a liminal period, a time when it can feel as though everything is up in the air. It can be disturbing, and there is a strong sense of not really being in control. Suddenly very different things seem important, and other things that did seem important suddenly become irrelevant.

One thing I almost always recommend to candidates discerning their vocation is to have a spiritual director or a soul friend, someone they can talk to in complete confidence about the whole of their lives and especially about what God is saying to them. This is important for several reasons. First, the whole process of discernment is about trying to listen to what God is saying to us, so it is often very useful to talk that through with an experienced individual who is good at listening and discerning the things of God. Second, the emotional turbulence that can come with a sense of call can be very strong, and it helps to have someone who will support you through that time. Third, you might want to share things that are personal to you with someone who is not part of the discernment process as a whole. Spiritual direction is, and should be, wholly confidential, a space to share whatever you like with another human being.

My experience is that those who are looking at being ordained benefit a great deal from a spiritual director or soul friend.[3] Apart from anything else, they provide a 'safe space', but they can also help an individual to find some of the language he needs to describe this extraordinary experience of being called: a language that it is necessary to articulate if you are to follow a discernment process through.

I know that it takes courage to say out loud, especially for the first time, 'I think that I might be called to be ordained' – particularly for young people when such a thing is so counter-cultural: it can feel like quite a risk. I still remember the moment I told my family, around the table at a meal: it felt a monumental thing to say. Their response was, 'We thought you could do something better than that', although I think they would say something different from that now!

A stay at a retreat house may offer a helpful time of quiet away from the storms of life to listen to what God is saying to you. Some houses have special rates for young people. You will probably benefit on such a retreat from having a guide you can speak to each day about how you're feeling and how the retreat is going. I have found that God rarely speaks out of the noise, but into the silence. Perhaps that is why Jonah ends up in the belly of a fish: enforced silence and solitude!

But Jonah's days in the belly of the fish are also strongly symbolic of how some experience the journey of discernment. It can lead us into dark places. Certainly it is not unusual at some point on the vocational journey to become despondent, or to wonder what is going on. Some become depressed. Vocation is such an intimate, personal thing that it is not surprising that it stirs the depths of our being, where much darkness is stored. Again, it can be good to have a wise person to speak to and support you during such a time.

It is certainly not uncommon, particularly when young people begin their ordination training, for some quite personal issues to arise: vocation is, after all, about who we are as a person. God has a tendency to lead us into very surprising places, and they are often, in my experience, places where it is hard to sense anything of God's presence at all. But looking back later, it can become very clear that God really was there after all.

In dark times as well as good times, this prayer by Thomas Merton can be particularly helpful:

> My Lord God, I have no idea where I am going. I do not see the road ahead of me. I cannot know for certain where it will end. Nor do I really know myself, and the fact that I think I am following your will does not mean that I am actually doing so. But I believe the desire to please you does in fact please you. And I hope that I will never do anything apart from that desire. And I know that if I do this you will lead me by the right road, though I may know nothing about it. Therefore I will trust you always though I may seem lost and in the shadow of death. I will not fear, for you are ever with me, and you will never leave me to face my perils alone.[4]

Then there is the ego. This is what I most love about Jonah: all that grumpiness. After all that running away, storms, the fish and then finally doing what he had been asked, he looks like an idiot. He's fed up. Angry. Despondent. He wants to be dead. In our current world, obsessed with targets and with so much emphasis on success, Jonah's story has a lot to say to us. Ultimately, I guess the message is that the journey of any vocation leads us to learn the importance of abandoning ourselves to God's will and his love. And that act of surrender is frightening: our ego kicks and screams at the idea of giving up power.

This prayer from St Ignatius of Loyola puts this very forcefully and courageously:

> Take, Lord, and receive all my liberty,
> my memory, my understanding
> and my entire will,
> all I have and call my own.
>
> You have given all to me.
> To you, Lord, I return it.

Everything is yours; do with it what you will.
Give me only your love and your grace.
That is enough for me.

I am reminded too of the famous quote of Dag Hammarskjöld: 'Night is drawing nigh – For all that has been – Thanks! To all that shall be – Yes!'[5] These words take courage both to say and to believe.

But perhaps this all sounds somewhat abstract to you and a little hard to grasp. To make it more real, here is a story from my own spiritual journey. While on a silent retreat once, I was feeling restless – as often happens to me on retreat. I was trying to work out what the future held for me, and how I could use what God had given me for his good. Round and round in my head the ideas went. Then, suddenly, I distinctly sensed a voice speaking to me that said: 'You could ask me!' The journey of discernment is precisely a frightening, exciting and courageous one because ultimately it is little to do with what we want: it is about what God desires for us. Often that simply doesn't make sense, at least at first, and sometimes never. But whoever said it would?

To quote St Paul:

For the message about the cross is foolishness to those who are perishing, but to us who are being saved it is the power of God. For it is written,

'I will destroy the wisdom of the wise,
and the discernment of the discerning I will thwart.'

Where is the one who is wise? Where is the scribe? Where is the debater of this age? Has not God made foolish the wisdom of the world? For since, in the wisdom of God, the world did not know God through wisdom, God decided, through the foolishness of our proclamation, to save those who believe. For Jews demand signs and Greeks desire wisdom, but we proclaim Christ crucified, a stumbling-block to Jews and foolishness to Gentiles, but to those who are the called, both Jews and Greeks, Christ the power of God and the wisdom of God. For God's foolishness is wiser than human wisdom, and God's weakness is stronger than human strength. (1 Cor. 1.18–25)

The following is a story from recent history that shows a man who learned, through what I sense was a great struggle, how to follow God's will, which led him to a strange place and eventually to a violent death.

John Bradburne was born in 1921 in England, the son of a Church of England clergyman. He served as an officer in the Gurkhas during the Second World War, in both Malaya and Burma. His life is a complete patchwork of different possibilities and ideas. He had a go at being a school teacher, and working in forestry. In 1947 he converted to Roman Catholicism, and in the years that followed he three times tried to become a monk. He also fell in love and almost married. He wandered around England doing various jobs: in the eyes of society he was a distinctly unsuccessful and unfocused human being.

When John Bradburne was nearly 40 years old he travelled to Africa, to see an old friend, Father Dove, who was in Rhodesia (now Zimbabwe). He stayed on, and eventually, after almost ten years of a similarly nomadic existence, he found through another friend a settlement of lepers at Mutemwa, and he lived and worked there for the rest of his life. The lepers endured the most dreadful conditions, but John worked hard to improve their lives and encouraged them to build a small church for the community. For the latter part of his life he lived as a hermit, while still caring for the lepers: a life of utter simplicity, praying, caring and writing poetry. He existed completely without any money. When war was raging in Rhodesia and the situation was getting dangerous, John ignored pleas from friends for him to leave. On 2 September 1979 John was kidnapped; his body was found on 5 September: he had been shot and killed.

The life of John Bradburne is a reminder that God rarely calls us to that which makes sense. The life of God's kingdom is necessarily different from that of the world. But this is really hard, particularly for those of us who live in a world that judges our work most often by our achievements and our success. John Bradburne's life looks like an utter failure, a waste both of his gifts and of his life, and yet many view him as a saint. The same could be said to be true for many who are called to be nuns or monks or hermits. To the world, their lives make little sense, but to those with eyes of faith the monastic life is one of the most spiritually subversive things you can be called to do. Richard North's book *Fools for God* brings out that theme beautifully.[6] Members of the Church of England are often surprised to find that we too have monastic orders. It is possible that God may be calling you to that vocation in life: if you feel that may be so, talk about it with someone you trust and try to arrange to visit a monastery. They are great places to visit – they are the most wonderful, best kept secret of the Church.

One of my colleagues here in Durham uses the image of the court jester to symbolize the ministry of a Chaplain in the university, the jester being the only one in a royal court who can tell the monarch the truth and yet survive. I like that image a lot, and I have often thought about how that rings true for my ministry: for instance, I am very lucky to be given the freedom not only to say grace at formal college meals but also to use whatever words I wish for that grace. I try to make it humorous, but usually there is a truthful sting in the tale. Using humour along with truth means that the truth sometimes becomes more palatable and accessible.

Sometimes I wonder whether we have lost the sense of mischief and play that jesters and clowns have – and in particular, whether we have allowed the modern media to place all who are in public life under such scrutiny that this type of eccentricity is hardly possible. No wonder we are all so anxious! To quote Thomas Merton, 'What is serious to me is often very trivial in the sight of God. What in God might appear to us "play" is perhaps what He himself takes most seriously.[7] Young people often bring that sense of fun, mischief and play to society in general and to the Church in particular; this can so often be a great gift, and release the ego from its self-declared importance.

Here's a lovely illustration of this from Roly Bain, a priest and clown:

> The clown embodies and offers a world where different rules apply, a world that has been turned upside down and inside out, a playful world where the only rules are the law of love. It's a place where everybody wins and everybody loses, all at the same time. It's the world where the first are last and the last first, so that when the first become last they become first again! But nobody's counting, because everybody counts – everyone is important and each is loved.[8]

One of our potential ordinands was having problems filling in his registration form for his Bishops' Advisory Panel. I went to see him in London and we met up in a parish office that happened to have a whiteboard. He was completely stuck on one question and getting more and more anxious about completing it. I suggested that we play with the question and just throw words out aloud connected to it. I wrote them all up on the whiteboard, and after a bit of time it became clear that the answer was there in front of us. Play, not effort, had revealed the answer.

Reflection

Even by biblical standards, given the fact that God seems almost always to call the least likely people, Jonah is an extraordinary choice for what God has in mind for him. The only other mention of Jonah in the Bible (in 2 Kings 14.25) suggests that he is someone more comfortable with putting borders in place to keep foreigners out than doing the opposite. This is precisely why he runs away on receiving God's call to go to preach in a distant foreign city, as he himself later admits: 'That is why I fled to Tarshish at the beginning; for I knew that you are a gracious God and merciful . . .' (Jonah 4.2). One of the ways we can recognize the authentic call of God is when we realize that we are being invited to step into a larger picture of reality, to work with and to pray for those we least like, or those who are most fully strangers to us.

But Jonah's decision to refuse God's call has serious consequences for others, as well as for him. It even has consequences for the created order: the result of his decision to take a ship to Tarshish, in exactly the opposite direction from Nineveh, is 'a mighty storm' (1.4). It's worth reflecting on what consequences there may be for the creation, the environment, when we – or all humanity – deliberately resist what God is calling us to do. In the book of Jonah, the consequences are, of course, most serious for the innocent sailors of the ship on which he is travelling. And we should notice Jonah's initial lack of interest: resisting our vocation risks turning us into narrow, self-centred individuals: 'What are you doing sound asleep?' cries the boat's captain, as the sailors struggle desperately to save themselves and Jonah too (1.6).

Yet it is at this point that Jonah comes to his senses. Like the prodigal son, he accepts responsibility for what is happening: 'Pick me up and throw me into the sea; then the sea will quieten down for you; for I know it is because of me that this great storm has come upon you' (1.12). His failure to respond to God's call leads him, paradoxically, to become an anticipation of Jesus, who declares that 'just as Jonah was for three days and three nights in the belly of the sea monster, so for three days and three nights the Son of Man will be in the heart of the earth' (Matt. 12.40). In our acceptance, even at the last minute, of our failure to be the people God wants us to be, our preference for narrow self-interest over God's generous compassion, we can become Christ-figures for others.

49

Jonah's prayer 'from the belly of the fish' (2.1) is also striking. He begins it with what we would expect to be its conclusion: a celebration of what God has done even before God has done anything at all ('I called to the LORD out of my distress, and he answered me', 2.2). It is characteristic of biblical prayer to anticipate – to celebrate what we would love to see God do, even before there is the remotest sign that God will do it; for by doing this we challenge the powers of apathy and evil. Jonah goes on to articulate the utter despair he experienced ('Then I said, "I am driven away from your sight; how shall I look again upon your holy temple?"', 2.4), and it is in the midst of this despair that God acts ('As my life was ebbing away . . . my prayer came to you', 2.7). Even in the furthermost extremes of desolation, God hears and answers prayer.

And so at last Jonah comes to Nineveh, the city he never wanted to see and certainly didn't want to see God care about. The most reluctant preacher in history is also the most successful: his peremptory and pessimistic preaching is stunningly fruitful. Why? No one has ever explained this better than Eugene Peterson:

> [When] Jonah entered Nineveh . . . he didn't make appreciative comments on the landscape; he let loose with something arrestingly eschatological: 'Yet forty days, and Nineveh shall be overthrown' . . . He didn't accuse them of being evil. He didn't denounce their sin and wickedness. He called into question their future. He introduced eschatology into their now-oriented religion, their security-obsessed present.[9]

Eschatology is the exploration of, and the endeavour to live into, God's new future. Jonah tells the Ninevites that they cannot go on as they are. It may well be that God is today calling people to proclaim exactly the same uncompromising truth to the world of the twenty-first century – and to do so precisely in places and among people that most of us are tempted to ignore or forget about. It's worth noticing that although God describes the Ninevite way of life as 'evil' (3.10), God doesn't blame them for this: rather, God describes them as not knowing what they were doing (4.11), just as Jesus will ask his Father to forgive those crucifying him 'for they do not know what they are doing' (Luke 23.34). Jonah looked on Nineveh and saw a nasty foreign city full of people he couldn't care less about; God looked on Nineveh and saw a society that could change and thrive, if only someone could help them to believe it.

The book ends with the famous image of the castor-oil plant (or some similarly obscure bush, 4.6). Sulking when he sees God have compassion on Nineveh, Jonah enjoys the shelter the bush provides, until it dies as abruptly as it appears (4.7). The bush represents two things at once: first, the trivia with which we concern ourselves when whole cities and societies are at risk; second, the fragile created order that keeps reappearing in the short book of Jonah – storms, whales, plants and animals, all of which are included in God's all-embracing compassion. The story of Jonah ends with a question that is also a challenge: God says to his grumpy and reluctant prophet, 'You are concerned about the bush, for which you did not labour and which you did not grow . . . And should I not be concerned about Nineveh, that great city, in which there are more than a hundred and twenty thousand people who do not know their right hand from their left, and also many animals?' (4.10–11). Vocation is not about the individual Christian's search for fulfilment, although the divine call offers us the way to a fulfilment far deeper than we could ever find alone; rather it is about God's urgent love for a created order, as well as a human race, in desperate need of healing and a new future. There will always be excellent reasons why we should leave this challenge to others, and book our passage to Tarshish, or preoccupy ourselves with personal or national or ecclesiastical trivia. But God puts the same question to us as God once put to Jonah: if I am concerned about the Ninevehs of my world, shouldn't you be too?

5

The counter-cultural nature of call

But Ruth said,

> 'Do not press me to leave you
>   or to turn back from following you!
> Where you go, I will go;
>   where you lodge, I will lodge;
> your people shall be my people,
>   and your God my God.
> Where you die, I will die –
>   there will I be buried.
> May the LORD do thus and so to me,
>   and more as well,
> if even death parts me from you!'

When Naomi saw that she was determined to go with her, she said no more to her.   (Ruth 1.16–18)

I have attended only a couple of civil partnerships, and this reading was used at a sung Eucharist to celebrate one of them – the civil partnership of some close friends – and I found it very moving. If the Christian journey of faith is about a love affair with God, then our exploration of our vocation is part of the story of that love affair. We discover something of who we are through others, and we learn in love to surrender ourselves to another – just as in our relationship with God we learn how to give our whole lives to the one who gave us life.

I think it's important to recognize that particularly in the early stages of falling in love, love really makes no sense at all. It is hard, if not impossible, to rationalize love – and so it is with our love affair with God. Sometimes he calls us to do the most extraordinary of things, things that make no sense whatsoever. It is there in the lives of the disciples. It is there in the lives of the saints. Look at how St Francis of Assisi's life was turned upside down by God's call. William Golding captured this very well in his book *The Spire*:

> The net isn't mine, Roger, and the folly isn't mine. It's God's folly. Even in the old days he never asked men to do what was reasonable. Men can do that for themselves. They can buy and sell, heal and govern. But then out of some deep place comes the command to do what makes no sense at all – to build a ship on dry land; to sit among the dunghills; to marry a whore; to set their son on the altar of sacrifice. Then, if men have faith, a new thing comes.[1]

Love leads us into odd and unexpected places. It is my strong belief and experience that God is calling young people to be ordained. As we have already explored, he often calls them from a young age. But it is sometimes hard for older generations to remember what it feels like to be called at an early age; it can be a very odd experience. It's not what most young people want to do! So finding the courage to put that into words, out loud, is quite something. It can seem like you're the only person in the world feeling this way. And young people don't come neatly packaged with a sticker attached saying 'potential priest'. One individual, who is now ordained, describes her first experience of being called:

> I first had a sense of calling to be in ordained ministry when I was aged about nine years. I was sitting in the back of my parents' car. My mother and father were in the front discussing the forthcoming General Synod vote on the ordination of women to the priesthood. Both were in favour of the vote passing. However, I, out of nowhere, had this gut-wrenching sense, as if I had just been punched in the stomach, that I might not be able

to do what I was being asked to do, that was to become a priest. Yes, I regularly attended church, but it really wasn't, nor did I expect it to become, a fundamental part of my life, and I certainly didn't want to work for it since I saw how flustered and annoyed my father would return home, who was at the time a church warden, after he had attended a PCC meeting. So, I simply tried to ignore this sense of being called to be a priest; it really wasn't something I wanted to do.

Looking back on my own life I can see that I owe a great debt to my father's younger brother Andrew. As I mentioned before, I come from Surrey, and members of my family have largely worked in the City of London. My father was a solicitor, my grandfather an accountant. The family mould was fairly clear – but my uncle, who had gone to Oxford to read medicine, decided while he was there to change course entirely and become an artist. It was a courageous decision, and not a popular one, particularly with the family. It carried huge financial implications for him, but he did it. While reflecting on my own vocational journey I have come to realize that his story has influenced mine: he gave me a sense, particularly when I was a child, that I could step out of our family narrative (or perceived narrative) and follow a path that felt truer to being myself. I suspect we all need people in our lives who model authentic living, be it relatives, friends or colleagues, or those we read about from history.

I am an avid film-lover, and for me the greatest vocation film is *Billy Elliot* (2000). It helps that it is based in the north-east of England, with its wonderfully rich spiritual history and incredibly friendly people. The film tells the story of a boy who has not only a hidden gift, but what turns out to be a calling to be a ballet dancer. As depicted in the film, a boy ballet dancer could not have been more culturally unacceptable, and yet it is clearly his vocation: it is what brings him alive. Stories like *Billy Elliot* have the potential to inspire people to be true to who they are, and to live lives closer to what they are called to be.

One candidate I saw for ordination, who is now ordained, I found so surprising that I almost had to pinch myself. I well remember my first meeting with him. He played rugby for the university. He was Head of Security for one of the colleges. He drank beer, a lot. And then he said that he read Theology, that he had been on retreat, and that he enjoyed the writings of Carl Jung, which was all a bit unexpected. It turned out that behind a persona of a confident sportsman and a bit of a lad was a young man with a deep inner life, and a close relationship with God – and above all a nagging sense that he was called to be ordained. It took great courage for him to tell his college chaplain, and then me, and even more to tell his college friends. But he did, and as his training for the priesthood progressed, and he was ordained, he had a profound impact on his friends, many of whom came to his ordination. As time has gone on, more and more of his friends and contemporaries have begun to understand why he has been ordained, and now turn to him with questions of faith, and for support when life is tough.

I have used the language of vocation as becoming what God made you to be, and finding the place where you can most become that. One quite obvious aspect of discovering more about who you are as a person is the realization that you are different from others, and to be true to that takes courage. To become the individual you are made to be means that over time you may begin to reject some of those things that society, family or advertising suggest you 'should' be – what psychologists might describe as the 'false self'. The pressure to be other than we are is enormous, not least for young people. Consciously and unconsciously, we receive the message that we need to be like everyone else, through advertising, the media and peer pressure. I remember talking about this one night with a candidate in the pub where we had just met; on the way home, he gave me a big hug and said: 'Thank you for being Jon.'

At a talk that I give in the University to Durham Nightline, I use this extract, written by a boy of 14, which speaks eloquently to me of the powerful forces of social conformity, and the difficulty of being true to ourselves:

He always
He always wanted to explain things,
But no one cared.
So he drew.
Sometimes he would just draw and it wasn't
    anything.
He wanted to carve it in stone
Or write it in the sky.
He would lie out on the grass
And look up at the sky
And it would be only the sky and the things
    inside him that needed saying.
And it was after that that
He drew the picture.
It was a beautiful picture.
He kept it under his pillow
And would let no one see it.
And he would look at it every night
And think about it.
And when it was dark
And his eyes were closed
He could see it still.
And it was all of him
And he loved it.
When he started school he brought it with him,
Not to show anyone, but just to have it with him
Like a friend.
It was funny about school.
He sat at a square brown desk
Like all the other square desks

And he thought it would be red.
And his room was a square brown room,
Like all the other rooms.
And it was tight and close.
And stiff.
He hated to hold the pencil and chalk,
With his arms stiff and his feet flat on the floor,
Still, with the teacher watching and watching.
The teacher came and spoke to him.
She told him to wear a tie
Like all the other boys.
He said he didn't like them
And she said it didn't matter.
After that they drew.
And he drew all yellow
And it was the way he felt about morning.
And it was beautiful.
The teacher came and smiled at him.
'What's this?' she said.
'Why don't you draw something like Ken's drawing?'
'Isn't it beautiful?'
After that his mother bought him a tie
And he always drew airplanes and rocket-ships
Like everyone else.

And he threw the old picture away.

And when he lay out alone and looking at the sky,
It was big and blue, and all of everything,
But he wasn't anymore.

He was square and brown inside
And his hands were stiff.
And he was like everyone else.
All the things inside him that needed saying
Didn't need it anymore.

It had stopped pushing.
It was crushed.
Stiff.
Like everything else.[2]

This moving piece reminds us of the destructive possibilities that come with social conformity: it ties in with the destructive nature of a thwarted vocation, discussed in Chapter 3. When we feel, for whatever reason, that we cannot become ourselves, this carries the potential for very negative consequences. That is why the exercise of the *examen* can be so helpful: we can use it to keep an eye on what is bringing us to life and what isn't. The journey towards being true to ourselves is both an outer and an inner one. The inner process involves a deep listening to what we feel called to be; the outer one involves discerning the different people and environments that allow us to be ourselves, or not. Social conformity and the pressures of family and society can be very powerful indeed. The film *Dead Poets Society* (1989), which has a lot to say about being true to yourself, brings that out very strikingly. As I have hinted from my own vocational story, ordination is not viewed by every family as the dream ticket for their child. Being ourselves can be immensely threatening to those who are not true to themselves. It reminds me of that extraordinary quote from Herbert McCabe: 'If you don't love you're dead, and if you do, they'll kill you.'[3]

So there is always something counter-cultural, radical and subversive in following our sense of call to be ourselves, because necessarily it will bring us into conflict with those who want us to conform. But that is where love can lead us, as the story of Ruth tells us so eloquently. Ruth herself is led to a foreign land, and to a new relationship of love with Boaz, a man from a different nationality from her own. And yet through this surprising call of love Ruth becomes a direct descendant of David.

In both hearing God's call for ourselves, and in helping others to hear what God is saying to us, there needs to be an openness to the unexpected, to that which is different, to the gift that so often comes in the thing that is alien to us and a complete surprise!

Reflection

We live in an age of migration, in which millions of people are in a constant state of flux, travelling in search of food, work, shelter and safety. In a sense, every age has been an age of migration, for the experience of leaving home in search of these basic necessities has characterized all human societies, and the lives of many other creatures too: salmon do it, caribou deer do it, birds do it, even butterflies do it. Migration is a natural, creaturely necessity that tends to be self-controlling: one might argue that what is unnatural is the erection of expensive borders in order to try and stop it. The great economist J. K. Galbraith once wrote:

> Migration is the oldest action against poverty. It selects those who most want help. It is good for the country to which they go; it helps break the equilibrium of poverty in the country from which they come. What is the perversity in the human soul that causes people to resist so obvious a good?[4]

The book of Ruth opens with a classic description of economic migration: Elimelech and his wife Naomi leave Bethlehem because of a famine and migrate eastwards to the country of Moab (Ruth 1.1–2). Then tragedy strikes: Elimelech dies, leaving Naomi with their two sons. Both of these take local Moabite wives, Orpah and Ruth; but ten years later the two sons die as well, leaving Naomi 'without her two sons or her husband' (1.5) – a solitary female migrant worker in a foreign land. Having heard that the famine back home in Judah has ended, Naomi prepares to return; but she tells her daughters-in-law to remain in Moab, their own land: after all, she is a widow with no more sons for them to marry. Orpah stays in Moab, but Ruth (as we have seen) insists on going with her mother-in-law, even though such a decision makes no rational sense. Ruth freely chooses to turn herself into an economic migrant and to leave home out of love for Naomi. And the two of them arrive in Bethlehem 'at the beginning of the barley harvest' (1.22).

God has barely yet made an appearance in the story, although Naomi assumes that God is responsible both for ending the famine (1.6) and for bringing calamity upon her (1.20–21). Yet Ruth's decision to go with Naomi is a profound experience of vocation, which, as we shall see, is blessed by God. The very absence of God at the point at which Ruth makes her decision is in itself important, for the story highlights an important truth: life is irreversible, and frequently appears random (although the story will also show us how what appears to be random at the time may later acquire great significance); and the spiritual question all of us must face is what we do with what we cannot control or choose. To put it another way: the test of any healthy spirituality is how far it helps us to cope with what we didn't expect or want to happen.

The story so far also reveals another important truth: the significance of names. In the Bible, names often indicate (or are explicitly oriented towards) the future. Hence various characters, such as Abram, Sarai and Jacob, receive new names for new stages of their journeys under God's direction. When the parents of John the Baptist announce that he is to be called John, their relatives complain: 'None of your relatives has this name' (Luke 1.61). But that is just the point: what matters about John is what his future is, not what his past was; and his name bears witness to that. In the story of Ruth, all the characters we have so far met have names, even though some of them (Mahlon and Chilion, Naomi's sons) die young and appear to have no future; but they reappear by name at the very end of the story (4.9), because Ruth's vocation is precisely to help create the new future they did not live to see. When Naomi and Ruth reach Bethlehem, the women of the town ask, 'Is this Naomi?' and she replies, 'Call me no longer Naomi [which means "pleasant"], call me Mara [which means "bitter"], for the Almighty has dealt bitterly with me' (Ruth 1.19–20). But no one ever calls her Mara, and she remains Naomi, for despite her understandable bitterness she does have a future after all.

The story of what happens to Ruth and Naomi is too well known to require description here. But several points are briefly worth noting. We are told that Naomi and Boaz are related by marriage (2.1); but neither makes any attempt to approach the other. It is the powerless foreign migrant, Ruth, who brings them together. And it appears to happen by chance: when Ruth goes to work in the harvesting, we are told that 'As it happened, she came to the part of the field belonging to Boaz', and that 'Just then Boaz came from Bethlehem' (2.3–4). 'As it happened . . . Just then' – this is the language of random circumstance. Yet Naomi sees the hand of God here: 'Blessed be [Boaz] by the Lord, whose kindness has not forsaken the living or the dead!' (2.20). Part of the subtle beauty of the story is the way God works through apparently random events, some tragic and others routine, in order to accomplish the divine purpose.

But there is a far more important point than that. When Ruth and Boaz make clear their desire to get married, Boaz explicitly declares that this is happening 'in order that the name of the dead may not be cut off from his kindred and from the gate of his native place' (4.10) – Mahlon, Ruth's first husband, who died childless, young and in a foreign land, is to find his own unfulfilled hopes brought to fruition posthumously through the love of Ruth for Boaz. Christian vocation and Christian priesthood are never just for the person called – never private, never even simply for those to whom the person called will minister directly. It is the almost inconceivable privilege of vocation to discover that we may bring blessings even on those who have gone before us, just as those who have died in faith and who pray for us now may bless us. God does not prevent appalling tragedy from striking Naomi and her little family; but God does open up an entirely new future in the most unexpected way. The only moment in the whole story at which God is the subject of an active verb is at its climax: 'So Boaz took Ruth and she became his wife. When they came together, *the* LORD *made her conceive*, and she bore a son' (4.13).

And notice the astonishing conclusion! Having courageously decided to leave home and travel with her mother-in-law to a strange land, having gone to work on the land and developed a relationship with the prominent and prosperous Boaz, having married him and borne a son, Ruth disappears entirely from the scene. When she bears her son, the women of the town say to *Naomi*, not to Ruth, 'Blessed be the LORD, who has not left you this day without next-of-kin' (4.14). *Naomi* takes the child and nurses it (4.16). Even more remarkable, it is not Ruth or Naomi or Boaz, or even God, who names the child (and we have seen how important names are in this story): '*The women of the neighbourhood* gave him a name, saying, "A son has been born to *Naomi*." They named him Obed; he became the father of Jesse, the father of David' (4.17).[5]

The end of this beautiful story takes us to the heart of the mystery of Christian vocation, especially (though not only) the vocation to priesthood. Ruth is the outsider, with no power or status, and only a very incipient faith. Yet she is the one whose call it is to help bring to birth new life and new hope, not only for her own family or for her dead first husband, but for the entire community – and even, in time, for the entire nation. Ruth does not do this alone; and as the story makes clear, it is God who enables her to give birth to that new life. Nonetheless her role is vital; and yet once it is accomplished, she disappears from the scene. Her work is done, and we see her no more. So with us. Like Ruth, we have the opportunity, at good times but even more at bad ones, to choose for ourselves a vocation that (although it may not be apparent at the time) is God's loving purpose for us and for others. That vocation will turn us into foreigners, require of us the willingness to leave home and travel light, in a way, and for a reason, that may not make much sense at all, even to those closest to us at the time. It will take us to unfamiliar places and people, but these will nonetheless prove to be full of potential (this is the point about 'the beginning of the barley harvest' in 1.22). In acting in partnership with others, and under God's gentle but enduring direction, we discover that our vocation is a call to help bring to birth new life that will transform the future both of ourselves and our loved ones, and of those in the place where we minister. But then we must step aside, and let God and those around us make that future their own.

6

The subversive nature of God's call

In the sixth month the angel Gabriel was sent by God to a town in Galilee called Nazareth, to a virgin engaged to a man whose name was Joseph, of the house of David. The virgin's name was Mary. And he came to her and said, 'Greetings, favoured one! The Lord is with you.' But she was much perplexed by his words and pondered what sort of greeting this might be. The angel said to her, 'Do not be afraid, Mary, for you have found favour with God. And now, you will conceive in your womb and bear a son, and you will name him Jesus. He will be great, and will be called the Son of the Most High, and the Lord God will give to him the throne of his ancestor David. He will reign over the house of Jacob for ever, and of his kingdom there will be no end.' Mary said to the angel, 'How can this be, since I am a virgin?' The angel said to her, 'The Holy Spirit will come upon you, and the power of the Most High will overshadow you; therefore the child to be born will be holy; he will be called Son of God. And now, your relative Elizabeth in her old age has also conceived a son; and this is the sixth month for her who was said to be barren. For nothing will be impossible with God.' Then Mary said, 'Here am I, the servant of the Lord; let it be with me according to your word.' Then the angel departed from her.   (Luke 1.26–38)

I wonder what your image of God is? It's a useful thing to ponder. No image, no words can ever fully capture God, but we tend to have a sense of what God is like, from Scripture, from our Christian tradition, and from our own experience. Sometimes we also experience a disconnect, something that commonly comes up in deep spiritual conversation. For instance, we say that we believe that God is all-loving; then we might describe how we think about a particular situation and maybe realize, or it is gently pointed out to us, that we are not talking about a very loving God after all.

This happened quite startlingly with my own spiritual director once. Something disturbing and disquieting had happened in my own life; it had been a great shock and I wasn't at all sure what to make of it. I shared what had happened with her. She gently said, 'Jonathan, have you talked to the God you love and deeply believe in about this?' Of course not! The God I believed in, who was my friend and who loved me beyond all my imagining, was not someone I had uttered a word to about this event!

I learned more about this on a long, silent retreat I went on a few years ago, in the Ignatian tradition. Ignatius recommends beginning a time of prayer by asking for a grace – like the grace to understand a biblical passage or to enter into it more deeply. Being the person I am, I would often sit down to pray, get myself 'in the zone', and off I would go in prayer, without asking God for anything. I would frequently feel that I wasn't getting very far, and then I would hear a niggling voice inside that reminded me that I hadn't actually asked for anything. So then I would ask, and quite often the prayer became deeper and sometimes God did reveal things to me. I know that it is really obvious, but asking God to help us with things, and in particular in discerning his will, seems a good thing to do! Before every meeting with a potential ordinand, I now try to pray for the grace of discernment.

The Jesuit William Barry is very eloquent about this. In his book *Paying Attention to God,*[1] he raises a question that is absolutely central to prayer. Why talk to God about things, when he knows everything already? Barry's answer is both simple and profound: we don't just suddenly 'create' intimacy. Intimacy comes by sharing ourselves, our whole selves with another. So talking to

God about what matters to us builds the intimate relationship with God for which God yearns.

The story of the Annunciation to Mary is one of the great descriptions of a personal call by God in our Christian tradition. But there has been, I fear, an enormous temptation to sentimentalize the story. My own realization of the importance of Mary has developed over time, but so has my lack of patience with how she is depicted in art, stained glass and statue. Too often she appears submissive, weak, or just not human! Many saints are depicted in this same way. I think it is worth spending some time reflecting and pondering on Mary's call.

Have you ever wondered: why Mary? Had God asked anyone else? What made her special? Is there a clue in the greeting of the angel Gabriel? 'The Lord is with you.' Does that not suggest that Mary was intimate with God? That through her way of life, and her prayer, she was already close to God, whether she knew it or not? 'The Lord is with you' seems to me an indication that Mary had a close relationship with God.

In church, I wonder whether we are aware of the power of the greeting, 'The Lord be with you'. When the angel greets Mary with these words, the angel is speaking to what we think was a teenage girl in a rather irrelevant town in Israel; the angel also declares to Mary that she is the 'favoured one'. Again we should perhaps ponder this phrase, in the light of how Mary's life pans out. Being pregnant when betrothed but outside of wedlock was a reason to be stoned to death in Jewish law.[2] So Gabriel's message immediately brings the potential for shame. Mary has to go into exile once Jesus is born, a refugee in Egypt, away from her home and family. She then watches her son grow up, during which time her husband dies; and then her son dies in one of the most torturous ways known to humankind. And she's the 'favoured one'! It makes you wonder what happens to the less favoured ones.

But I cannot help feeling that Mary is an exemplar of vocation because of her attitude to what is unexpected and unimaginable. And in Mary we find another clue about prayer becoming clear. For years I found it hard to get my head around why we needed to ask God for things in prayer when he knew what they were already. Then I read a book that reminded me that God never forces himself on us – Christopher Bryant's *The River Within*.[3] And as it says in the book of Revelation: 'Behold, I stand at the door and knock; if any one hears my voice and opens the door, I will come in to him and eat with him, and he with me' (Rev. 3.20, RSV). God doesn't kick the door down. So prayer, in effect, oils the hinges of the door of our hearts, to let God in more and more. It goes back to that sense of surrender to God's will mentioned in Chapter 4. When we are open to God, grace flows. I wonder if that was so with Mary: that she was open to the things of God, which because they are of God are so often deeply surprising, if not startling. Maybe that is why we call Mary 'full of grace'. Maybe I also learned something about that on my long retreat: not only being open to God, but giving him the opportunity to be part of my prayer and my life by inviting him in.

I am attracted to this quote by Kathleen Norris from her book *Amazing Grace*, when she reflects on the story of the Annunciation:

> Mary proceeds – as we must do in life – making her commitment without knowing much about what it will entail or where it will lead. I treasure the story because it forces me to ask: When the mystery of love breaks through into my consciousness, do I run from it? Do I ask of it what it cannot answer? Shrugging, do I retreat into facile clichés, the popular but false wisdom of 'what we all know'? Or am I virgin enough to respond from my deepest, truest self, and say something new, a 'yes' that will change me forever?[4]

This is similarly expressed by the late Maria Boulding in her book *The Coming of God*. She says of the Annunciation:

> Like the prophets and the anonymous believers before her, she [Mary] let go of the familiar, intelligible patterns and

ways of relating to God and the universe, of those frame-
works which had genuinely supported meaning hitherto,
and were indeed God-given. She said her 'Yes' to the Beyond,
she let go of her securities, faced the misunderstanding, bore
the shame, accepted her own bewilderment and risk. She
was herself reborn to a new existence, that she might bring
forth life for many. There was joy for her, and in newness
of life she danced with the Beyond that was within.[5]

It reminds me of that scene in the Indiana Jones film *Indiana
Jones and the Last Crusade* (1989), when Dr Jones is trying to get
to the Holy Grail before his father dies. He stands at a cliff edge
and has to take 'the leap of faith' into the unknown. Our journey towards what God wants us to be and become requires that
level of courage and faith and trust. And because God does not
force himself on us, it requires a 'yes' from us, as it did from Mary,
no matter how hushed or scared we might be in saying it.

So here in the story of the call of Mary is a simple but important point: a call demands a response. In many respects the
journey of discerning our vocation under God consists of simply
saying 'yes' to God's will, and trusting where that will lead us.
'Thy will be done', we say in the Lord's Prayer; it's a dangerous
and courageous thing to say!

This is one priest's memory of experiencing God's love before
she began exploring ordination. She describes learning something about surrendering herself to God:

. . . one day when revising for my exams sitting alone next to a
river on a beautiful summer's day, I completely from nowhere felt
so happy, and I know this sounds crass, but I became aware that
I was loved. I felt I was loved for my foolishness, for my stubborn-
ness, for my imperfections, for basically just being me. And this love
towards me was being unconditionally emanated from something
I couldn't grasp or understand, but was completely precious, in other
words God. I remember, probably looking like a complete nutter

to those who passed by, since I was sitting by myself, howling with laughter, and repeatedly uttering the phrase 'I have kicked the baby out with the bath water'. I realized that previously I had told God who she was, either she was a teacher and I was her favourite, her pet, but when she expected me to do something I didn't want I instantly rejected her, and turned her into a non-existent tyrant, and I had never just let God be God and simply have the courage to relish and delight in the mystery of it all.

It is also worth dwelling on the consequences of saying 'yes' to God. Mary did not know what accepting God's will would bring – just as we do not. It brought her shame, discomfort, risk to her life, and grief, as well as, we imagine, joy and inspiration. There should be some small print on any vocational literature warning that following a sense of call is risky; and there is a temptation, I suspect, in all of us to assume that God has called us only to do the things that we want to do. I have been surprised, looking back on my priestly ministry, to discover that some of the most exciting and fulfilling parts so far have been working with people and in places I would never have thought to find myself. One example would be schools. I was told by a friend, a fellow curate, when I was first ordained that schools were where ministry was at. He was someone I really trusted, so I started visiting local schools; despite a latent fear that I would be no good and wouldn't enjoy the experience, before long I was taking assemblies. This was all new to me, and I feel sorry for those who had to undergo my first attempts. But soon I came to love my work in schools; I discovered that I really enjoyed it, and it bore much fruit.

I have recently noticed a shift in attitude in many of the friends of the candidates I see: their fellow students seem supportive and encouraging of their sense of call. In an age where employment is a big issue, and the amount you are paid can become more important than whether you actually enjoy what you do, I sense that a lot of young people are in awe of one of their peers having such a clear understanding of what they want to be. But I have witnessed very hostile reactions from some parents. While this may always have happened, being a 'Vicar' nowadays is not seen as a position of status in a community, nor as a particularly noble thing to do. I have some sympathy with that: my parents paid a small fortune for my education, and now I simply have a stipend, not a job in the City with a salary to match like some of my friends. But the call of God is neither to respectability nor to material gain.

However, it is important to take seriously the difficulties a young potential ordinand might be experiencing by going against the expectations of her family and in particular her parents. The attitude that being ordained is not a 'proper job' can put you under a lot of pressure, whether you know it or not. It can also emphasize any internal sense you have that 'people like me don't get ordained'. Most parents want what is best for their children, but only we can live the life we have, and follow the calling that we might have too. As we explored earlier, stepping out of the family's expectations for us takes courage, and if that is the case, it is good to have support in other places to help us.

Speaking of support, another thing to point out about Mary is that she was the person she was because of her life experiences, not least the care and love she received from her parents, Anna and Joachim. We are who we are through the care, love, challenges and battles we experience in our interaction with others. Mary was formed through many influences, consciously and unconsciously, and it was because of these influences that she could say 'yes' to God. It was because of her love and care for Jesus that he could discover who he was and who he was called to be.

Many people have contributed to make you who you are – and me who I am. Every so often it is worth pondering this in prayer, and thanking God for all those who have helped to give birth to the person we are. Perhaps that is also a prayerful way of reflecting on the genealogies we find in the Bible. I have the idea with vocation that there is a barely visible thread that runs through a sense of call, informed by many generations of people who helped make you you, and me me. I also feel strongly these days that we ourselves may be an answer to many prayers: somehow we are their fulfilment, as Mary was to the hopes and aspirations of generations in Israel, praying through so many centuries for the One who was to come.

This is one of my favourite quotes (and I have many!), which somehow captures that thought for me. It is attributed to Pablo Casals:

> Every second we live is a new and unique moment of the universe, a moment that never was before and never will be again. And what do we teach our children in school? We teach them that two and two make four and that Paris is the capital of France. We should say to each of them: 'Do you know what you are? You are a marvel. You are unique. In the millions of years that have passed, there has never been another child like you.'

Mary also reminds me of another important theme regarding vocation. A friend once suggested that we are a multiplicity of vocations. Mary was called by God to be a mother, a wife, a faithful follower of God, a friend, as well as many other things. Very often in life a particular vocation comes to the fore. But it is especially important for young candidates to remember that friendship is also a vocation, as is family life; and for those who are married, marriage is a vocation as well. I don't believe in a hierarchy of vocations, but at certain points in our lives some will need more attention than others. Even within ordained ministry there are many different vocations.

We have seen in this chapter that it is the life of prayer – our own, and the fruits of others' prayer – that is at the heart of the vocational journey. Discovering how to be intimate with God, how to come close to him, and how to surrender to him are part of a lifetime's journey. For this reason there is one book that I consistently recommend to those thinking about ordination: Evelyn Underhill's *Concerning the Inner Life*.[6] It is short, which helps!

It is also starkly honest about the importance of prayer in the life of a Christian minister. Here is a glimpse of what she says:

> And what you are like is going to depend on your secret life of prayer; on the steady orientation of your souls to the Reality of God. Called upon to practise in their fullness the two great commandments, you can only hope to get the second one right if you are completely controlled by the first. And that will depend on the quality of your secret inner life.
>
> Now by the quality of our inner lives I do not mean something characterised by ferocious intensity and strain. I mean, rather, such a humble and genial devotedness as we find in the most loving of the saints. I mean the quality which makes contagious Christians; makes people *catch* the love of God from you.[7]

Of all the different aspects of my role with potential ordinands, the greatest is the privilege of having these young candidates sharing with me that deep inner life: a life that is often so closely guarded and well hidden in people of their age. A vocation to ordained ministry is very much about developing that inner life as well as the outer life of active ministry, as Evelyn Underhill so disarmingly makes clear. That deep inner life is what sustained Mary through the unpredictable vocation of her outward life, and is what I imagine Luke fleetingly refers to when he states, 'But Mary treasured all these words and pondered them in her heart' (Luke 2.19).

Reflection

As pattern and exemplar of Christian vocation, the Virgin Mary presents a paradox. On the one hand, her vocation is unique to her: no one else's vocation, however important, has ever been to give birth to 'the Son of the Most High' (Luke 1.32). On the other hand, there is one sense in which the vocation of every single Christian is based upon hers, for we are all called to incarnate, to give birth to, the love of God in Christ in our own unique situations. And it is precisely her humble self-abasement in the face of so exalted a vocation that makes her exemplary.

And not only her self-abasement. Mary's response to the angel's call, especially if seen in the light of Old Testament precedents, reveals a person at once humble and strong. She does not ask for, or receive, any kind of sign or miracle, unlike most of the Old Testament characters who were called by God. She does not go and look for her fiancé, in search of male reassurance, when she hears what the angel has to say – unlike the unnamed wife of Manoah and mother of Samson (Judg. 13.6). She does not accept her vocation without question, as Rebekah and Rachel did, nor does she laugh incredulously at the thought of it, as Sarah did (Gen. 18.12). Instead she explores its implications boldly and thoughtfully, as men like Gideon had done (Judg. 6.13): 'she was much perplexed by [the angel's] words and pondered . . . [and she] said to the angel, "How can this be . . . ?"' (Luke 1.29, 34). It's intriguing that she appears much more interested in the *means* by which this conception is to take place, than in the answer to the question most of us would have posed first: 'Why me?' Where Zechariah, in Luke's first Annunciation story, demands proof on being told he is to be a father late in life (Luke 1.18), Mary demands information: as Augustine points out, 'she believed, but she was asking about the manner of it' (Sermon 287:4). She does not doubt the call; she does not ask to know what its consequences will be for her, or what others will think. Instead she probes and ponders, but then responds with all she has to give: 'Here am I, the servant of the Lord; let it be with me according to your word' (Luke 1.38). It may be the same with us – we need some idea of what our sense of call will mean in practice, and with it some of Mary's confidence that an authentic call from God can be questioned and explored before we give it our full-hearted assent.

What follows is equally striking. Mary sets out to visit her cousin Elizabeth, who is pregnant with John the Baptist: when

Mary greets Elizabeth, the unborn baby leaps for joy (Luke 1.44): once accepted, and even before its implications can possibly have been grasped, one genuine vocation evokes recognition in another, each, so to speak, authenticating the other. And this leads at once to Mary's famous Magnificat, in which she imagines her own vocation being in some sense replicated everywhere, with the lowly lifted up and the proud dethroned – as though poor and lowly people everywhere will resonate with her call, and feel God's astonishing new life being conceived within them, as Elizabeth had done. Mary *out-imagines* the harsh social structures of her day, dreaming into being a different kind of world. This is no narrowly private call, but a word of radical hope for all humanity. And it may be that a vocation from God needs both these kinds of authentication – first, some spark of answering recognition from someone similarly called; and second, an imaginative recognition that *my* call must in some way find expression in the lives of those 'on the edge'.

In the light of this, it isn't surprising to find Scripture reminding us that Mary's vocation was to be anything but easy. Simeon's sombre warning to her, that 'a sword will pierce your own soul too' (Luke 2.35), is given added weight when the 12-year-old Jesus goes missing during a visit to Jerusalem, and is found talking with the religious teachers. Mary's agonized protest ('Child, why have you treated us like this? Look, your father and I have been searching for you in great anxiety' (Luke 2.48)) articulates with unsurpassed power the experience of all whose sense of vocation suddenly confronts them with a hard truth: the God who calls us, and whose love, like Mary, we seek to bring to birth, is in no sense our private possession, and will come and go for reasons that may not be clear to us. Mary has to experience the terrible pain of the real absence of Christ just when she must have come to take for granted his real presence. Yet this real absence is not a rebuke: rather, Mary has to allow her perspective to be enlarged. She has to let go of self, not once but over and over again, as when Jesus tells those around him that all who hear the word of God and do it are his mother and his brothers (Luke 8.21). It's not about her; and, in the final analysis, it's not about us either.

Which brings us to Mary's second Annunciation, for she has not one but two. The second takes place at the foot of the Cross, when she has to prepare to experience the real absence of her son in the most appalling way imaginable – by watching him die (John 19.25–27). She says and does nothing: she is, simply and unconditionally, there, doing what the sleepy and frightened disciples in Gethsemane had failed to do: to keep Christ company. The image of Our Lady of Sorrows embodies the despair and anguish of countless people after her, Christians and others too, whose sense of vocation and youthful hopes appear to be consumed in unspeakable tragedy. Yet it is at just this moment of dereliction that the crucified Christ opens up a new future, both for the bereaved mother and for his closest friend. And he does this by inviting each to see, to discern, that new future in one another – the King James Version's 'Woman, behold thy son!' and 'Behold thy mother!' is closer to the original than the NRSV's dull 'Woman, here is your son ... Here is your mother.' From that act of mutual recognition, that discernment, or beholding, of hitherto undreamed-of new possibilities in two people whose vocations had seemed to end in disappointment and death, the Christian Church is born.

That leads us to Mary's last appearance in the pages of the New Testament. Luke describes the apostles after Jesus' ascension, 'constantly devoting themselves to prayer, together with certain women, including Mary, the mother of Jesus, as well as his brothers' (Acts 1.14). *'Perseverantes unanimiter in oratione'*: the Latin translation of this verse from the Vulgate Bible will have influenced countless Christians, not least those responding to a call to the monastic life, in the centuries following the earthly life of Christ. It is striking that Luke mentions Mary here by name, perhaps to underline the fact that the woman who alone was present at the conception of the one who was to be both her son and her Lord was also present at the birth-pangs of the Church that would be his living body on earth after his ascension. Whatever the reason, this text is one of the richest in Scripture for our understanding of vocation. First, it underlines that Christian vocation can never be purely private or purely public: it will always embrace both, always engage the whole of ourselves. The presence, at the dawn of the Church, of the woman who was closest to Jesus' private life, together with the apostles who were closest to his public life, is a vivid image of this profound truth. Second, the image of Mary and the apostles 'constantly devoting themselves to prayer' reminds us of the corporate nature of our vocation, and of its originating focus in the life and worship of the Church, Christ's body. It is in our baptism, and our participation in that shared life and worship, that our own call finds its truest expression. Third, this text reminds us that all vocation is rooted not in activism, or in the discharge of professional skills or ecclesiastical roles, but in alert, expectant, open-hearted prayer. And there is an even more important point still.

Mary is the person whose freely chosen obedience to God's call makes possible what for Christians is the most astonishing event in history since the creation of the universe: the Incarnation of the Son of God. The fact that the evangelist (Luke), who tells us about this, also describes her by name as being present at the birth of the Christian Church suggests not only that this event too will be world-transforming, but also that all Christian vocation is about an invitation to share in God's amazing, unpredictable, life-changing work of renewing our world. Why? Because, as we have seen, we are invited, like Mary and with her, to bring the love of God to birth. We cannot know, any more than she did, where our acceptance of that invitation will take us. But we can believe, incredible as it may seem, that our modest 'yes' to the call of God will give our lives a meaning they could never otherwise have had, and make of us, as it made of an obscure young woman from Nazareth, part of a divine and loving purpose beyond anything we could have imagined.

7

God's call and failure

In the year that King Uzziah died, I saw the Lord sitting on a throne, high and lofty; and the hem of his robe filled the temple. Seraphs were in attendance above him; each had six wings: with two they covered their faces, and with two they covered their feet, and with two they flew. And one called to another and said:

'Holy, holy, holy is the Lᴏʀᴅ of hosts;
the whole earth is full of his glory.'

The pivots on the thresholds shook at the voices of those who called, and the house filled with smoke. And I said: 'Woe is me! I am lost, for I am a man of unclean lips, and I live among a people of unclean lips; yet my eyes have seen the King, the Lᴏʀᴅ of hosts!'
Then one of the seraphs flew to me, holding a live coal that had been taken from the altar with a pair of tongs. The seraph touched my mouth with it and said: 'Now that this has touched your lips, your guilt has departed and your sin is blotted out.' Then I heard the voice of the Lord saying, 'Whom shall I send, and who will go for us?' And I said, 'Here am I; send me!' And he said, 'Go and say to this people:

"Keep listening, but do not comprehend;
keep looking, but do not understand."
Make the mind of this people dull,
    and stop their ears,
    and shut their eyes,

so that they may not look with their eyes,
and listen with their ears,
and comprehend with their minds,
    and turn and be healed.'

Then I said, 'How long, O Lord?' And he said:

'Until cities lie waste
    without inhabitant,
and houses without people,
    and the land is utterly desolate;
until the LORD sends everyone far away,
    and vast is the emptiness in the midst of the land.
Even if a tenth part remains in it,
    it will be burned again,
like a terebinth or an oak
    whose stump remains standing
    when it is felled.'
The holy seed is its stump.

(Isaiah 6)

Some years ago I was doing the washing up with a bishop, as one does. He said at one point, 'Jon, do you know what the definition of a saint is?' 'No, Father,' I replied politely, 'you tell me.' 'Someone whose life hasn't been properly researched,' he replied, with a grin.

As explored in the previous chapter, Mary, along with many saints, and God himself, suffers from our projections, and those of the Church and of others, both now and through the past centuries. Some particular projections, and pressures of our age, make authentic living a courageous act indeed. But not just that: there are huge pressures on us to be successful and to be perfect. When an Archbishop of Rowan Williams' calibre can be criticized in the public press for the size of his eyebrows, you get a sense of where we have got to.

That pressure is felt by many potential ordinands, as discussed in Chapter 3, who voice the sense of fear that they are not up to being a priest. I want to explore this further in this chapter, and to link it to the deep inner freedom that I believe God longs for us to experience.

Years ago I went to see a therapeutic counsellor who happened to be a Roman Catholic priest. He told me that at one time when he was in parish ministry he had felt desperate and suicidal. After his Christmas break he spoke to his bishop, and said in desperation, 'I really cannot go back to this parish.' The bishop replied, 'Well, don't.'

I rather like that story. It could be misunderstood – but I don't think it illustrates a get-out clause for things we simply don't want to do. Rather, it is a graphic illustration of how we often box ourselves in, cause ourselves to feel trapped: and that constraining is usually simply of our own making. We become victims of our own 'oughts' and 'shoulds'. My understanding is that Jesus' good news is not only about deep inner freedom and liberation, but about total reliance upon God. That is why the story in the Endnote of this book by Martin Laird is so powerful: it speaks to me of the freedom that comes from knowing God's love deep down in my inner being. A love that means we have nothing to prove.

But so many of us, and I include myself here, either consciously or unconsciously feel that we have something to prove. A former spiritual director used to say to me, 'God draws, and the devil drives.' Our drivenness may come to life in an addiction to our work or obsession with our achievements, which in themselves can become forms of idolatry. Eugene Peterson usefully reminds us that saying 'no' is an act of liberation; in effect, this is what the bishop in the story above was recommending. Peterson goes on:

> Grammatically, the negative, our capacity to say No, is one of the most impressive features of our language. The negative is our access to freedom. Only humans can say No. Animals can't say No. Animals do what instinct dictates.

No is a freedom word. I don't have to do what either my glands or my culture tell me to do. The judicious, well-placed No frees us from many a blind alley, many a rough detour, frees us from debilitating distractions and seductive sacrilege. The art of saying No sets us free to follow Jesus.[1]

Later he states: 'Busyness is the enemy of spirituality. It is essentially laziness. It is doing the easy thing instead of the hard thing. It is filling our time with our actions instead of paying attention to God's actions. It is taking charge.'[2]

It's useful to reflect on a culture that has created a sense that worth comes only through success and achievement, and where work-alcoholism is not only accepted but often modelled by those who are high achievers. That is not the focus of this book, and others have gone into the subject in great depth. I can speak from personal experience, however. As I mentioned earlier, I went on a long retreat a few years ago, and I spent close to a month in silence. Many unexpected things happened on that retreat, but one that I found particularly surprising was that I watched, almost on a daily basis, my emotional defences slip away. They weren't really needed, I suppose, and I found myself opening up and becoming more generous in disposition and nature, as well as increasingly aware of my own weakness and fragility. At the heart of the gods that we create, and fall down and worship, is perhaps the fear that without them we might simply feel that we are worthless and of no use. We hide ourselves behind walls of success and achievement in case others might see who we really are.

This can be summed up in a piece of writing from my university days; I also use it in my talk at the Durham Nightline training weekends:

> Don't be fooled by me!
> Don't be fooled by the masks I wear:
> Masks I am afraid to take off.
> NONE of them is me.

I give the impression that I am secure,
Within and without,
That I am confident,
That I need no one.

Smooth though my surface seems,
Surface is my mask.
Beneath dwells confusion, fear, aloneness,
Nobody must know my weakness:
I create a nonchalant, sophisticated façade
Behind which to hide
From the knowing glance
Which would be my salvation.

I fear that glance –
It might not be followed by acceptance and love.
I am afraid that you will laugh at me instead.
I am afraid, deep down, that I am worthless.
I am afraid that you will reject me.

I dislike this superficial game of words I play.
I want to be genuine and spontaneous,
To discover myself.

I need your help.

Please hold out your hand to me,
Uncaring, ungracious, ungrateful though I seem,
Please offer me kindness, and encouragement.

A long conviction of worthlessness builds
Walls, thick and tall.
Love is stronger than walls, I am told.

Please beat down these walls,
With firm, but gentle hands,
For your child is very sensitive.

It is very easy to become trapped in a way of being in which
we feel that we constantly have to prove our worth, by what

we do and how we are – and this is particularly true of ordained ministry. John Sanford, in his book *Ministry Burnout*, perceptively gives the example that clergy often get involved in building projects in their parishes so that they will have at least one demonstrable thing to show for their efforts.[3] It can be hard, if not impossible, to see what if anything we have achieved in ministry. That's the nature of it.

But again, this striving for achievement is in fact ego worship. For me, liberation has come slowly but powerfully through the example of people who are prepared to be really honest about who they are, and in doing so have not asked for pity or attracted attention. Such people include Michael Mayne, Judy Hirst and Jean Vanier; and in particular Mark Townsend in his book *The Gospel of Falling Down* and Vanessa Herrick and Ivan Mann in *Jesus Wept*.[4] Actually the starting place for responding to God's call is empty hands. We have nothing to offer except the very selves God breathed into being.

It's difficult to describe, but Martin Laird's story in our Endnote does so very well. But the greatest thing about beginning to get a sense of this liberation is how it simply doesn't fit into the idea of power structures and status. Jean Vanier told a story that summed this up for me when I heard him speak in Edinburgh a few years ago. He described a somewhat miserable day when he was in Paris. He was in the metro subway, in some pain as his back was hurting, and he went past a beggar, who shouted insistently at him. Jean went to speak to him. The beggar suddenly looked Jean in the eye and said to him: 'We're in the same boat, you and I,' and Jean Vanier replied, 'Yes, we are.' How tempting I would have found it to say something like, 'No, we're not, we're quite different.' There's a reason Jesus was born in poverty: he could never be above anyone else in status. He could therefore always remain a genuine friend, a companion to those without status or position. We can also find the presence of Christ quite clearly in those in poverty and in need, as Jean Vanier states:

Those who come close to people in need do so first of all in a generous desire to help them and bring them relief; they often feel like saviours and put themselves on a pedestal. But once in contact with them, once touching them, establishing a loving and trusting relationship with them, the mystery unveils itself. At the heart of the insecurity of people in distress there is the presence of Jesus. And so they discover the sacrament of the poor and enter the mystery of compassion. People who are poor seem to break down the barriers of powerfulness, of wealth, of ability and of pride; they pierce the armour the human heart builds to protect itself; they reveal Jesus Christ. They reveal to those who have come to 'help' them their own poverty and vulnerability. These people also show their 'helpers' their capacity for love, the forces of love in their hearts. A poor person has a mysterious power: in his weakness he is able to open hardened hearts and reveal the sources of living water within them. It is the tiny hand of the fearless child which can slip through the bars of the prison of egoism. He is the one who can open the lock and set free. And God hides himself in the child.

The poor teach us how to live the Gospel. That is why they are the treasures of the Church.[5]

If you're not feeling up to the call of God, the best resource I can recommend is the DVD *Dust* by Rob Bell.[6] It makes a very powerful point, which is well put and in the end simple: look at who Jesus chose to be his disciples. They weren't 'the best of the best', as Rob Bell puts it – quite the opposite. He also didn't call them to a glamorous life either. But he called them.

Liberation can be found, I think, in the deep recognition that ministry is God's ministry; his call is for us to be part of that, to celebrate with others what we see God doing in our lives and in the lives of others and in the world, and to join in. When the focus is on God, then necessarily we concentrate less on us.

The late Canon John Fenton put this very forcibly:

It [St Mark's Gospel] is the best book for the twenty-first century because it is so utterly subversive. Western European culture will need some subversive people to do something about its capitalism and its love of self. The one character who is the model in Mark's Gospel is the child and the child is there as a representative of people who are unskilled, nobodies: who have no status. The child appears twice, in chapter 9 and chapter 10, and in both cases Jesus hugs them. They are the only people that he does hug. The rich will find it hard to enter the kingdom of God. The first will be last and the last will be first. Life will be through death; death will be the only way forward. This will be necessary for the twenty-first century, when what we will all be trying to do is to live as long as possible and be as rich as possible. But notice one thing about this rich man: he wants to know what he should do. He has kept the commandments and Jesus says he lacks one thing – 'Sell what you have and give to the poor', and the man goes away sad. And it says there in Mark, 'Jesus looked at him and loved him.' It is the only instance of Jesus loving somebody. He loves the person who can't do it. This again is subversive and this is what is so good about Mark. He saw that his readers would never be able to accept his book, and he was right . . .

We see the impossibility of the demand, 'Destroy your life! That's the only way to preserve it.' And we know we can't do it . . . but the man who couldn't do it was the one that Jesus loved. Away success. Welcome failure! That's the good news.[7]

The reading from the Bible we have chosen for this chapter, if looked at closely, speaks about failure. Gordon explores this further below, but the famous story of the call of Isaiah, although initially inspiring in the first few verses, goes on to forecast a ministry of complete failure – and the strange mystery of failure is that it has the potential to open us up to God's grace. To face reality. It breaks the powerful walls of the ego and persona. It gives us the grace to allow God in. This is what Richard Rohr has to say on the subject:

> After working with people as a priest for over 31 years, I have come to an extraordinary conclusion: we come to God not by doing it right, but by doing it wrong. This is obvious to me now, although it does not become obvious until the second half of life. By then, if we are honest, we have seen the pattern in ourselves and in others. You understand mercy and grace by looking backwards. Looking forwards it is just a nice theory, but not yet 'good news'.
>
> Why, then, are we so obsessed with the bad news of being right? Why do we spend so much time trying to concoct a worthy ego?[8]

Alongside the temptation of the desire to be successful is the desire to be perfect – the perfect ordinand, the perfect priest, the perfect Christian, the perfect person. Again, the media presents us with images of 'perfect' people, advertising 'perfect' clothes and a 'perfect' way of life with 'perfect' friends. Some find this pressure to be perfect crippling. It is certainly detrimental to us spiritually. There is another quote I like, again from Richard Rohr:

> In a Navajo rug there is always an imperfection woven into the corner. And interestingly enough, it's where 'the Spirit moves in and out of the rug.' The pattern is perfect and then there's one part of it that clearly looks like a mistake. The Semitic mind, the Eastern mind (which, by the way, Jesus would have been closer to) understands perfection in precisely this way.
>
> Perfection is not the elimination of imperfection. That's our Western either/or, need-to-control thinking. Perfection,

rather, is the ability to incorporate imperfection! There's no other way to live: you either incorporate imperfection, or you fall into denial. That's how the Spirit moves in or out of our lives.[9]

Much of this comes to the fore in prayer. It is a common assumption, particularly in those outside the Church, that prayer makes you feel 'better'. In my experience it does sometimes, but more often than not it unsettles. Prayer, and especially silent prayer, can seem a very vulnerable place: one where we can stand metaphorically, or even in actuality, naked before God. Stripped of everything. It's no wonder that St Francis of Assisi began his new Christian life by publicly removing all his fine clothes.

Carol Carretto discovered something of this truth when he went to the desert to pray:

For many years I had thought I was 'somebody' in the Church. I had even imagined this sacred living structure of the Church as a temple sustained by many columns, large and small, each one with the shoulder of a Christian under it.

My own shoulder too I thought of as supporting a column, however small.

Through repeating that God needed men and the Church needed activists, we believed it.

The structure was a burden on our shoulders.

... now I was here, kneeling on the sand of the cave, which had taken on the dimensions of the Church itself; on my shoulders I could feel the small column of the activist. Perhaps this was the moment of truth.

I drew back suddenly, as though to free myself from this weight. What had happened? Everything remained in its place, motionless. Not a movement, not a sound. After twenty-five years I had realised that nothing was burdening my shoulders and that the column was my own creation – sham, unreal, the product of my imagination and my vanity.

I had walked, run, spoken, organised, worked, in the belief that I was supporting something: and in reality I had been holding up absolutely nothing.

The weight of the world was all on Christ Crucified. I was nothing, absolutely nothing.

It had taken some effort to believe the words of Jesus who had said to me two thousand years earlier: 'When you have done everything that is commanded you to do, say, "We are unprofitable servants, because we have only done our duty"' (Luke 17:10).

Unprofitable servants![10]

I wonder, then, whether in this chapter we have seen a movement – a movement that on the journey of discernment and in ministry we often need to be reminded of – shifting the focus from our own endeavours towards watching, noticing, celebrating what God is doing. Discernment of vocation then becomes something that we notice God is working on within us; others may notice this too, and celebrate. It ceases to be something that we feel we 'do'.

Holy people often laugh a lot, not least at themselves, and I feel that this is no accident. This quote by Harry Williams might give us all hope. He says that it is '[when I am able to] laugh at myself that I accept myself, and when I laugh at other people in genuine mirth that I accept them'. He goes on:

Self-acceptance in laughter is the very opposite of self-accusation or pride. For in the laughter I accept myself not because I'm some sort of super-person, but precisely because I'm not. There is nothing funny about a super-person. There is everything funny about a man who thinks he is.

In laughing at my own claims to importance or regard I receive myself in a sort of living forgiveness which is an echo of God's forgiveness of me. In much conventional contrition there is a selfishness and pride which are scarcely hidden. In our desperate self-concern we blame ourselves for not being the super-person we think we really are. But in laughter we sit light to ourselves. That is why laughter is the purest form of our response to God . . . For to sit light to yourself is true humility. Pride cannot rise to levity.[11]

When we gain a true sense of our own poverty, as well as the fact that God loves us beyond anything that we can imagine, then we have what you might call 'startled joy': even I can serve God, and he can work through me, even me, if I let him!

Reflection

The story of Isaiah's call, in the sixth chapter of the book that bears his name, is probably the grandest and most transcendental description of a call to be found in Scripture. It begins with a startling subversion, continues with one of the classic accounts of true worship – and it all ends in failure.

The subversion comes first. 'In the year that King Uzziah died, I saw the Lord sitting on a throne' (6.1). We are not being told this simply for reasons of chronological precision, but because Isaiah wants to contrast two very different kinds of kingship, and to make it clear which takes precedence for him. Political rulers like Uzziah will come and go, but Isaiah wants to say: I am accountable to a higher and holier king than them, and if I have to choose between them I know which one comes first. Descriptions of this kind are not uncommon in the Bible – the wonderful story of the prophet Micaiah, standing alone before not one but two earthly kings, and defying them in the name of our heavenly king, contrasts a true prophetic vocation with that of a whole crowd of self-serving pseudo-prophets who grovel to the two earthly rulers and tell them only what they want to hear – and the story also manages to poke fun at the two kings for sitting in all their royal finery in the middle of a farmyard! (1 Kings 22.1–40). And the even more subversive story of Shadrach, Meshach and Abednego defying the seeming omnipotence of the Chaldean king Nebuchadnezzar, even though that defiance causes them to be pitched into the burning fiery furnace, contains one of the greatest passages in Scripture: 'If our God whom we serve is able to deliver us from the furnace of blazing fire and out of your hand, O king, let him deliver us. But if not, be it known to you, O king, that we will not serve your gods and we will not worship the golden statue that you have set up' (Dan. 3.17–18). What is distinctive about Isaiah's challenge to his earthly ruler is that it takes place in *worship*; and this gives to all true worship an inherently subversive character, for it is precisely there that we enthrone a higher and holier king than the Caesars of our own day.

Which brings us to Isaiah's famous description of worship (Isa. 6.1–8). Its first and primary ingredient is *adoration*, the offering of unconditional love and reverence to God without expecting anything in return. Adoration is thus intrinsically subversive: think of the adoration of the Magi, which outrages the local political ruler because it enthrones a higher power than he. Equally importantly, adoration lifts us out of self: to offer unconditional love and reverence to someone else is to enthrone that person, rather than ourselves, as the focus of our attention. It reminds us that fundamentally worship is not about us. Evelyn Underhill writes that, unfortunately, worship tends to 'decline from adoration to demand, and from the supernatural to the ethical'.[12] As it is described in Isaiah's vision, adoration lifts the worshipper into an alternative view of reality, giving the individual a glimpse of the transcendental glory of God that relativizes our view of the visible cosmos. Adoration releases the imagination that frees us to dream of a different world. What is, in utilitarian terms, entirely useless is precisely the key and mainspring for personal and corporate change. It drives

Isaiah down to his knees: 'Woe is me! I am lost, for I am a man of unclean lips; yet my eyes have seen the King, the LORD of hosts!' (6.5).

My father died when I was 16 and my brother was 14. In an attempt to cheer us up, my mother arranged for the three of us to go to Geneva for a week's holiday over Hogmanay. It proved a mistake. The city and the adjoining lake were shrouded in dense, gloomy fog all the time we were there. On our last day, desperate to find some way to lighten the mood, my mother spotted a bus going to Montreux, at the other end of the lake, and we set off: perhaps it would be sunnier there. It wasn't. But there was a funicular railway, ascending a mountain called the Rochers de Naye. In the fog? It seemed crazy, but we went. It was an unforgettable experience. As we went up, the little train emerged from the cloud and fog into a wonderworld of sunshine: people were laughing, sitting outside drinking beer, and skiing, while across the lake the snow on the summit of Mont Blanc sparkled. Another world had been there, above us but easily accessible, all week, and we hadn't realized. That is what adoration does for us in worship: it lifts us into a different world, which exists all around us all the time, if only we realized it was there.

The other ingredients of worship in the vision of Isaiah are more briefly described. His *repentance*, or acknowledgement of unworthiness, leads to his experience of *forgiveness*, which is mediated sacramentally: the seraph touches his mouth with a live coal – a rather uncomfortable experience: 'Now that this has touched your lips, your guilt has departed and your sin is blotted out' (6.7). Why his lips? Because he is about to be called by God to be a prophet, and the prophet's primary resource is his or her speech. The words we speak or write can take on a life of their own, for good or ill; and if they are spoken in the name of the God who declares through Isaiah that that word 'shall not return to me empty, but . . . shall accomplish that which I purpose' (55.11), they can change lives for ever.

Adoration, repentance and forgiveness: together these three ingredients of all true worship lead directly to the fourth: *commissioning*, or sending out. 'Then I heard the voice of the Lord saying, "Whom shall I send, and who will go for us?" And I said, "Here am I; send me!"' (6.8). Most readings of Isaiah's vision stop there, with the prophet's courageous response to his vocation. But that is to miss the whole point of the vision, for God at once proceeds to make clear that Isaiah's call to be a prophet and a preacher is not going to achieve anything much ('Go and say to this people, "Keep listening, but do not comprehend; keep looking, but do not understand." Make the mind of this people dull, and stop their ears . . .' (6.9–10a).) No one has ever described this terrible moment better than Eugene Peterson:

> As Isaiah is pulled into the holy life and finds himself involved in holy work, he is at the same time told that nothing much is going to come of it [6.9–10]. He is to be a preacher but a conspicuously unsuccessful preacher. He is going to preach with incredible power and eloquence and people are going to go to sleep in the middle of his sermons. It will turn out that he will have access to King Ahaz, be an insider to the operations of statecraft, and will have his wise and godly counsel ignored. The end result of a lifetime of God-ordained and God-blessed preaching is that the country will be destroyed – 'utterly desolate' [6.11]. The Assyrians are going to march in and ravage the place. It is going to look like a forest that has been clear-cut by rapacious loggers – ugly, defaced, barren – all the trees cut down and hauled away with nothing left but stumps, an entire country of stumps. 'This is what is going to happen, Isaiah, after a lifetime in my service. This is the end result of your immersion in holiness, your honest confession and cleansed speech, your vocation in holy orders. Stumps. A nation of stumps.'

But there is more to the stump than anyone supposes: 'A shoot shall come out from the stock of Jesse, and a branch shall grow out of his roots' [11.1].[13]

Christian vocation is not only, or even primarily, a call to the honing of professional skills, or the achievement of targeted objectives, important though these things can be. It cannot simply be measured by outcomes, or authenticated by instant success. It is a call to failure because it is an invitation to walk the way of the Cross. Walter Brueggemann has pointed out the striking fact that all four Gospels include God's sombre prediction that Isaiah's prophecy will achieve nothing (Matt. 13.14–15; Mark 4.12; Luke 8.10; John 12.37–43), but not one of them cites Isaiah's famous 'Here am I; send me.' Why? Because the experience of the early Christian Church was itself an experience of failure: huge numbers of Jews and Gentiles refused to join it, or to heed the gospel of the resurrection. Yet from the small shoots that sprang from all that failure was born a movement that could one day change the world. St Paul points to the heart of what a vocation to join that movement entails:

As God's ministers, we try to recommend ourselves ... by innocent behaviour and grasp of truth, by patience and kindness, by gifts of the Holy Spirit, by unaffected love, by declaring the truth, by the power of God ... Honour and dishonour, praise and blame, are alike our lot: we are the impostors who speak the truth, the unknown men whom all men know; dying we still live on; disciplined by suffering, we are not done to death; in our sorrows we have always cause for joy; poor ourselves, we bring wealth to many; penniless, we own the world.

(2 Cor. 6.4, 6–10, REB)

8

'Let anyone who has an ear listen to what the Spirit is saying to the churches'

————•◦•————

(Revelation 2.29)

The same night [Jacob] got up and took his two wives, his two maids, and his eleven children, and crossed the ford of the Jabbok. He took them and sent them across the stream, and likewise everything that he had.

Jacob was left alone; and a man wrestled with him until daybreak. When the man saw that he did not prevail against Jacob, he struck him on the hip socket; and Jacob's hip was put out of joint as he wrestled with him. Then he said, 'Let me go, for the day is breaking.' But Jacob said, 'I will not let you go, unless you bless me.' So he said to him, 'What is your name?' And he said, 'Jacob.' Then the man said, 'You shall no longer be called Jacob, but Israel, for you have striven with God and with humans, and have prevailed.' Then Jacob asked him, 'Please tell me your name.' But he said, 'Why is it that you ask my name?' And there he blessed him. So Jacob called the place Peniel, saying, 'For I have seen God face to face, and yet my life is preserved.' The sun rose upon him as he passed Penuel, limping because of his hip.   (Genesis 32.22–31)

Meaning does not come to us in finished form, ready-made; it must be found, created, received, constructed. We grow our way toward it. And sometimes the precious bit of true self, the unlived bit of soul, hides in psychological complexes, in illness, even in tragedy, even in sin. Hence the compelling idea of *felix culpa*, the happy sin that is an occasion of grace. Some mysterious power uses what we see as horrific and as the defeat of all our hopes to bring about our salvation.[1]

There is a huge difference between a job and a vocation. A job is what we hold to earn money to meet economic demands. A vocation (from the Latin *vocatus*, calling) is what we are called to do with our life's energy . . . We do not choose a vocation; rather it chooses us.[2]

The Holy Spirit is always making the new out of the old. I am amazed as I read the history of the Church with its pains and struggles. Always new things unfolding: new prophets, new saints arising to announce the old truths, but in new ways. There is always a tension in the Church between the old and the new: supporters of the old are fearful of the new and see it as a threat, as dangerous and wrong; they condemn it and sometimes even destroy it. The initiators of new ways can also be angry with the old, rejecting it as wrong, as corrupt or evil and then breaking away from it. Similar tensions exist in every community, and as each one evolves according to the inspirations of the Spirit and the needs of the time but is reluctant to change.[3]

Some years ago, when I first became a vocation adviser in Durham Diocese, I went to the National Vocation Advisers' Conference organized by the Ministry Division in the Church of England. At one of the workshops, we were asked how we might find more young vocations for ordained ministry in the Church of England. In the group I was in, I said in my familiar and somewhat provocative way that I felt that this was the wrong question to ask. I felt that the 'right' question was: 'Is God still calling young people to be ordained?' If the answer was 'no' then that was relatively straightforward; if the answer was 'yes', then the question might become, 'How can the Church better foster and nurture young vocations?'

That question has been the motivation for this book. My experience suggests that God is calling young people, a lot of young people, to be ordained in the Church of England, but much still needs to be done to foster and encourage those young people in discerning God's will for them. That is not to discredit those already doing that work: quite the opposite. It is to celebrate that work and to encourage others to do the same. 'The LORD longs to be gracious to you' (Isa. 30.18, NIV) is a phrase that often echoes around my head in relation to the Church and vocation.

Some years ago I watched a very moving documentary about a Roman Catholic priest who had been thrown out of the Church for being gay. The film ended, if I remember correctly, with him standing outside the Vatican. He said something like: 'When it comes to the end of days, I have a vision that the Church will stand before Christ and say: why didn't you send more labourers for the harvest? And Christ will turn to the Church and say: what did you do with the ones I sent you?'

The care and nurture of vocation is at the heart of the Church's work. And like any work that involves listening to the story of how God is working in a person's life, it is holy ground. It can therefore be extremely fragile, and needs to be handled with care and thoughtfulness, and also with encouragement and acceptance. A vocation that is heard, received and celebrated can in itself be life-giving.

It is rare that a sense of vocation arrives with absolute clarity and certainty as a bolt from the blue, although sometimes that does happen. More often, though, it is like a kind of wrestling match with God – as Jacob wrestles with an unknown being, as described in Genesis, who turns out to be God. Similarly, we ourselves can feel as if we are fighting, struggling and wrestling with something at the core of our being that often feels unattractive or repulsive; and when we make peace with it, we discover that has been of God, or is God. A vocation takes time, often lengthy amounts of it, to come to any sense of clarity. The road of discernment to a sense of call contains many challenges, struggles, sacrifices and surprises. It is the same for the Church, as she struggles to listen to what God is saying to her, and to discern her vocation under God. Necessarily, a call to ordained ministry has to be tested – as human beings, our powers of self-deception are really quite strong. The Church therefore has a role both in nurturing and fostering vocations to ordained ministry, and in discerning whether a person, through conversation, prayer and experience, has what others see as demonstrable evidence of a call.

The process for discerning a vocation to ordination in the Church of England is a rigorous one. It is often difficult for candidates to come to terms with the idea that it is not a competitive interview process, and that Bishops' Advisers and their colleagues are not there to trick people into giving 'the wrong answers'; rather, they are there to share a journey of discovery. That sharing of the journey is a great privilege because it is such a personal and intimate process. But because it is so personal and intimate, the fears of rejection, and of not being 'heard' or understood, are also very strong.

This book is very much about encouraging the nurture and formation of young vocations, so I haven't written until now about the experience of not being recommended. Clearly this is a possibility: not everyone is recommended who goes to a Bishops' Advisory Panel – although contrary to popular belief there is no quota to be filled for those to be recommended and those not to be recommended. Generally, dioceses have become increasingly careful about choosing candidates to send to National Panels, and that is, I would suggest, a good thing: not being recommended at a Bishops' Advisory Panel is an extremely painful experience, and it is a decision they do not make lightly.

A non-recommendation is often about timing – about being at the right place on the journey at the right time. By that I mean that it is particularly important to have begun to find the language to express the inexpressible or unutterable: the sense of God's call. It's also important for young candidates to be able to give an idea of their potential for some of the criteria for ordination – where because of their age they cannot evidence that by experience, for example.

Sometimes, although it is rare in my experience, it seems that those representing the Church don't hear the same call as that heard by the individual. This is important stuff. As a friend of mine puts it, it is part of the Church's role to speak honestly and truthfully if she discerns that a candidate is called to be something other than an ordained minister – it is in no one's interest, Church or individual, to do what God isn't calling you to do. We're then back to Jonah!

Usually there is something to learn from non-recommendation. You might be reading this now and smarting at such a patronizing comment. How on earth does he know? But the truth is that I was not recommended by my own Diocesan Panel back in 1989. I can still remember the words that were used to tell me the news (in a letter), and how I felt as a result. But in hindsight it taught me a lot about my behaviour: what I had said and how I came across in the interviews. It challenged me to think about how I communicated to others what I knew was in my heart; it also made me think about how other people experienced me. The odd thing about a selection process is that people who have never met you before need to get a measure of you in a very short period of time – and we ourselves can help or hinder that.

However, the Church isn't perfect (thank God), and does make mistakes. Whatever place in the discernment process you are at, there will always be times of struggle and lack of clarity, even, or especially, when you think it's all sorted. That is the same for the Church. In her processes and procedures the Church in particular needs to be open to the holy fools and spiritual jesters of this world: it is easy to create systems that spot just what we want, rather than what God desires. The Church has always needed those who test the boundaries, who dare the Church in the name of Christ to see visions bigger than she sees and take risks that might seem ridiculous but are what faith demands. It is worth considering whether some of those described in this book – those whose stories of vocation from the Bible are reproduced here – would be recommended for training for ordination in the Church of England. Would Jesus, for that matter! Gerry Hughes provides a good and imaginative reflection on this in his classic book *God of Surprises*.[4]

The Church needs ministers to represent her, to fulfil the duties of a minister, and serve the people of this nation. However, each of us is individual and unique, so we also need a Church that is open to the other, to the different, and to that which annoys us. In our risk-averse society we need an institution that is prepared to take risks, to go to exciting places with unpredictable people – if that is what God is calling us to be and do. That is, of course, frightening because it can mean change, and change often worries us. But the dance that is vocation is one that continues to re-mould and re-shape us, and by doing so changes those around us.

At the launch of 'Call Waiting', the Church of England's ongoing initiative to encourage young vocations, Rowan Williams told a story from Michael Ramsey's biography. In his last days, Michael Ramsey was visited by the owner of the local post office, near to where he lived in Oxford. The Muslim shopkeeper asked him how long he had been ordained. 'Nearly sixty years,' replied Ramsey. 'That's a very long friendship,' replied the shopkeeper.[5] Williams commented that vocation was important whatever our age – but the Church needs priests who have had a long friendship with God. Indeed.

Reflection

The story of Jacob wrestling in the darkness at the Jabbok ford is one of the most mysterious in the Bible. The person he wrestles with refuses Jacob's request to reveal his name: he is described simply as 'a man' (Gen. 32.24). Yet the man gives Jacob a new name, Israel, and tells him that he has striven with God and with humans and has prevailed (32.28). Or has he? Jacob leaves the place wounded, 'limping because of his hip', which was injured during the wrestling (32.25, 31).

What's going on here? A few points may be worth making. First, the location. Jacob has sent his family across the ford of the Jabbok (32.22): the Jabbok river is to play an important part as a boundary in the Old Testament, and here it clearly marks a key crossing point – Jacob is now committed to a crucial encounter with his brother Esau. This story is not the beginning of Jacob's vocational journey, but it represents a vital stage on that journey. For all who respond to the divine call there will be Jabbok crossings to make – moments in our lives when we have to make a key decision from which there is no going back; experiences or issues from our past that have been left unaddressed and need resolution; opportunities to move forward into a new but uncertain future that, if missed, may not recur.

And there's something else. The Jabbok crossing reminds us of an important truth about vocation: however much it is true that Christian vocation is always a call *into* the Body of Christ, into a particular role within that body, for which (as Jonathan points out above) we cannot avoid some kind of process of discernment and authentication, it is also true that that vocation is always in some sense a call *out*, out of our comfort zones into a place where we are exposed and sometimes lonely. It is striking that, at the very start of his own ministry, Jesus came out from Nazareth to be baptized by John in the Jordan (Mark 1.9). The Jordan was for Jesus what the Jabbok was for Jacob and the Rubicon for Julius Caesar: the river is a crossing point, a commitment from which, having been made, there could be no drawing back. And it is 'just as he was coming up out of the water' that Jesus hears the voice of his Father: 'You are my Son, the Beloved; with you I am well pleased' (Mark 1.10–11). Jesus hears a voice saying words to him that millions of children (and adults) in the world never hear from anyone: that he is unconditionally loved. The whole purpose of the Christian Church is to make that same unconditional love known and accessible to those who have never known it. It is in the assurance of that love that he finds courage to go forward. But having crossed the river of baptism, nothing could ever be quite the same again.

So with us; and so with Jacob. He is 'left alone' (Gen. 32.24), albeit by his own choice. In the final analysis, we have to make our own Jabbok crossings: no one else can do this for us, just as no one can do our dying for us. Yet he is not alone: at this moment of maximum exposure, in the darkness, someone assails him. Who is the assailant? It could be a dreamlike anticipation of the brother he has wronged and is about to meet again; it could be his own alter ego – those shadowy parts of his own self that he has sought to repress or flee from; or it could be an angel, obliging him to confront and engage with the demons he would much prefer to avoid. Or – and this is surely the most likely – it could be a combination of all three. What is clear is that the struggle bears fruit, even though it is costly: Jacob emerges wounded, but with a new name and a new future. He himself points to the meaning: 'I have seen God face to face, and yet my life is preserved' (32.30).

The story of Jacob at the ford of the Jabbok takes us to the heart of what we might call the spirituality of Christian vocation. Since that vocation will always be a call to the whole of ourselves, not just to one part, it will invariably involve a searching, often painful, opening up of everything that makes us who we are: our background, our sexuality, our unhealed hurts, our deep inner need both to give and to receive unconditional love. That process may take place as we make our initial response to our sense of call or it may come much later, after years of appearing to keep everything safely under control. For Jacob, it came when he could defer no longer the facing of a part of his past (his relationship with his brother) that he had hitherto avoided. In the event, his brother welcomes him with the same grace and generosity as the father with the prodigal son in Jesus' parable; but Jacob could not have known that during the long night at the Jabbok ford. He could have run away: he had done that twice before in his life (see Gen. 27.41—28.5 and 31.1–24). He could have decided to face his brother with guile and bravado, rather than a longing for reconciliation. He does neither. He faces his demons; he will not release the forces with which he is struggling until he receives some kind of blessing from them. He wrestles alone in the darkness with his fears and his failures, and somewhere in the midst of them he finds God, a new name and a new way forward.

A final point may be worth making. The Bible presents Jacob as a deeply flawed person, certainly not conventionally religious. He is courageous, capable of giving and receiving great love, yet also devious and sometimes self-serving. But it is precisely this fallible human being to whom God appears and whom God blesses and calls by a new name. And the sign, the clearest mark, of that blessing and authentic call is not a prodigious display of gifts but a wound: after his encounter with God he will walk with a limp (32.31). If the Church is truly to discern those whom God is calling to minister in its name, it will need to look beyond the concerns of institutional security and watch for the wounded prophets, the holy disturbers, the fallible risk-takers who may speak for God more credibly than any ecclesiastical manager or 'safe pair of hands'. This is easy to say but difficult to practise: in a time of economic recession, of ever-increasing exposure to the risk of litigation whenever anything goes wrong, and of complex employment legislation, there will be enormous pressure on the Church (and on all institutions) to select those who will not rock the boat, rather than those whose character or ethnicity or sexual orientation may well lead them to challenge the very Church that is calling them. Furthermore, there will always be, as there always has been, a creative tension between the priestly and prophetic vocations within the Body of Christ. Nonetheless, a Church that shies away from recognizing the vocations of a Jacob or a John the Baptist will soon find that it has nothing at all to say to the world and the society in which it is set.

At the Jabbok brook Jacob receives a new name: Israel. This apparently incorrigible individual, always prone to putting his own interests first, is given the name of the new people that God longs to call into being. Authentic vocation is always an invitation into a larger vision than self-interest. The Cistercian monk Thomas Merton once wrote:

> If self-will narrows us down and encloses us within a privacy that is too small to permit real growth of interior freedom, it is clear that unselfish devotion to a common cause is one of the ways in which our freedom and personal autonomy are best able to develop and to mature.[6]

Here is the greatest paradox of a Christian view of vocation: that an unconditional and costly commitment to put self second and to follow Christ offers the possibility of a level of fulfilment infinitely greater than can be had by seeking only what suits *me*. In that call, and in the assurance, albeit often fleeting and intermittent, of being secure in the love of the God who calls me, I am free: free from unconscious conformism to someone else's expectations of me; free from fear of the stranger or the 'other' who is not like me; free too from the need to submit to some narrowly churchy stereotype of what a Christian or a priest should be like. Having faced both his God and his demons at the Jabbok ford, Jacob was free to go forward to face his brother and to live into the new future to which God was calling him. And that radically unselfish interior freedom to be, and to become, the unique person God has created us to be is the surest sign of an authentic vocation, both in Jacob's day and in ours too.

Endnote

The stories that have been used in Jonathan's sections of the book are true; they have been anonymized, and appear with the permission of the individuals concerned. He is indebted to those individuals for allowing him to share these stories with others.

The two stories that follow are designed to prompt our imaginations, a key theme of this book. The first is from Martin Laird's *Into the Silent Land*, and has been referred to in this book; it is about vocation and our life in God.[1] The second is by David Mair, Head of Counselling at Birmingham University, and challenges us very specifically to think about how our world is constructed, particularly in relation to those who might be different from ourselves. Our encounters with those pondering and discerning their vocation will necessarily be about listening to something different from our own experience (since each of us is unique), and this meditation is designed to help us think about how we might be open to experience a context different from our own, and the effects that might have on a person growing up in that context.

'Who am I?' A tale of monastic failure

Abba Poemen said to Abba Joseph, 'Tell me how to become a monk.' He said, 'If you want to find rest here below, and hereafter, in all circumstances say, Who am I? and do not judge anyone.'   (Sayings of the Desert Fathers)

PART ONE

There was once a young man who didn't have the foggiest notion of what he wanted to do with his life. One day he said to himself, 'I know what. I'll enter a monastery, but not just any monastery, I want to enter a real monastery.' So off he went determined to find a real monastery. He came to the first monastery he could find and knocked on the door. The porter answered the door and said to the young man, 'Good afternoon. How may I help you?'

The young man said, 'I'd like to enter a monastery, but it's got to be a *real* monastery; is this a *real* monastery?'

The porter towered over him and pierced him with his dark eyes. He said to the young man, 'I'm sure you'd be more than welcome here, but I'm afraid I shall have to tell you we're not a real monastery at all. We're a fake monastery, you see. We're only pretending. So if you've got your heart set on a real monastery, I'm afraid you'll have to carry on down the road a bit until you come to the real monastery. You'll come to it before long. Now off with you. There's a good fella.'

The young man was delighted. He bade the porter farewell and set off down the road to find the real monastery. Soon he came to a large sign pointing down a small road that led into the woods. The sign read, 'Real Monastery 100 Yards'. Rubbing his hands in excitement, he followed the little road into the woods.

He knocked on the door, and the porter of the monastery soon answered. 'Good afternoon. How may I help you?' The young man's jaw dropped in amazement. He was certain it was the very same monk who was the porter at the fake monastery just up the road. The young man said, 'I'd like to enter a *real* monastery.'

The porter clasped his hands together and said, 'Well, you've come to the right place. Just come right in, and I'll take you down to the novitiate. I'm sure something can be arranged.' On the way the porter explained to the young man how fortunate he was not to have fallen for that fake monastery up the road.

The young man settled into the novitiate with relative ease. He found he liked all his fellow novices and pretty much all the monks he came across. It wasn't long before he felt certain he wanted to stay here for the rest of his days. So he went to the novice master and said, 'I believe I'm ready to make my profession.' The novice master said, 'Well, the abbot will have to see you about this.'

In due course an appointment with the abbot was arranged, and the young man sat down to speak with the abbot about his vocation. The abbot asked him why he felt he was ready to make his profession. The young man said, 'Well, I've come to like it here very much. Everyone is nice to me, and I like all the monks.'

The abbot said, 'Well, that is very encouraging to hear, and I'd have to say that we are very happy to have you and we hope that you stay. But just the same, I think you should go back to the novitiate for a while longer. It'll do you no harm.'

The young man left in great distress. Why didn't the abbot want him to make his profession? Did he say something wrong? Was he deluded about his vocation? Not a little disappointed, the young man returned to his life as a novice. The abbot's gentle rebuff ended up teaching the young man a great deal about his own faults and failings and presumption. He began to grow in self-knowledge and applied himself with great dedication to the study of the monastery's long history, its traditions, and various customs. He soon mastered all of this.

After more than a year the young man was convinced that now he would be able to answer correctly any question the abbot might put to him, and he could see, moreover, the abbot's wisdom in putting him off for a time. And so the young man told the novice master that he felt he was now ready to make his profession and could he please see the abbot. The novice master arranged this, and soon enough the young man was brought to the abbot.

The abbot said, 'I'm very happy to hear that you still want to make your profession and to live out your monastic life among us. But tell me, why do you feel you are ready to make your profession?'

The young man responded, 'I'm convinced that this is what God is asking of me. I don't claim to understand it. I only know it is something I must do. Moreover, I have been studying our tradition and our charism. I identify with it very deeply and think it confirms the sense of interior call that I feel.'

The abbot was obviously listening to him very intently and sincerely. He said to the young man, 'What you say is very edifying indeed, and I feel even myself encouraged in the life just listening to you speak the way you do about your conviction of God's love for you and of his call. But I think you should go back to the novitiate until you are really ready.'

The man was in quite a state as he left the abbot's office. He was in fact completely shattered. He couldn't imagine what on earth the abbot could possibly have wanted to hear. He knew he belonged more in the monastery than half of those other wretched monks. But he returned to the novitiate. He had already completed his formal studies, so he took to helping in the garden, pruning vines and thinning carrots, and also served in the infirmary.

He carried on with these jobs for what seemed like years. One day the abbot asked the novice master, 'What about that man who was so intent on making his profession in our monastery. Is he no longer interested?'

'He doesn't mention it much any more,' said the novice master.

'Is he unhappy?' asked the abbot.

'No, he seems content enough,' responded the novice master. 'He doesn't say much to anyone. He goes about his tasks in the garden; he consoles the old monks in the infirmary, and encourages the new ones in the novitiate.'

'Bring him to me,' said the abbot.

The man was brought to the abbot who began to question him: 'I was wondering if you were still interested in making your profession. You don't seem as keen to do it as you once were when you were making such a thorough study of our tradition. Have you gone off the idea altogether?'

The man looked at the abbot. The lines beginning to show round the man's eyes reflected the fact that he'd been in the monastery a number of years now. But his face had the freshness and peace of those whose poverty had taught them they had nothing to defend. The man said to the abbot, 'Jesus Christ is my monastery.'

The abbot sat up in his chair and leaned forward. He gazed into the man as though looking for something, looked into him as though gazing into the heart of mystery. His gaze fixed on the man, sifting him, assessing every turn taken, every decision made in order to know if this man really knew what he had said. The abbot stood up slowly, towered over him and said, 'You have learned our tradition well. May I have your blessing?'

PART TWO

After this man's second request for profession had been turned down and the abbot had sent him back to the novitiate until he was truly ready, he was in complete despair. This last rejection had unleashed within him a flood of swirling anxiety. He was seen working quietly around the place, but in fact he was only keeping up appearances; underneath his novice robes were spasms of chaos that would assault him like pounding waves. Once the chaos within was churning, it was all he could do to keep putting one foot in front of the other and somehow just manage to hold on. When the spasms of chaos let up, he would merely try to catch his breath and hope against hope that this was the last of these tidal waves of fear and panic. But it never was. Weeks became months. He realized he needed help, but to whom could he go? The novice master was allergic to life, and his regular confessor was completely switched off. There were 150 monks in the monastery. Who could help him? A certain Fr Alypius eventually came to mind.

Fr Alypius was something of a maverick, but he was thought to be wise. He was the cobbler and more or less lived in his little shop down at the bottom of the garden. He rarely spoke to anyone. It was said that he could read people's hearts, so everyone stayed away. The young man said to himself, 'I've got to go to him.' The next day at prayers, he left a note in Fr Alypius's place in chapel. 'Can I talk to you about something?' By early afternoon he got his reply. 'Come to me this evening after supper.' So after supper he crept down to the bottom of the garden to speak with Fr Alypius.

Crouched over a table, Fr Alypius was sitting on a stool repairing someone's shoes. He peered over the top of his spectacles and said, 'Sit down and tell me what's wrong.'

The young man went on for an eternity. He told him everything about his life, about his search for a real monastery, about his refusal for profession. All the while Fr Alypius was working away on this one shoe. When the young man had finished, Fr Alypius said, 'I have just one question for you: "who are you?"'

'I just told you,' said the young man.

'No, you told me about the clothes you wear. You told me your name, where you're from, what you've done, the things you've studied. Your problem is, you don't know who you are. Let me tell you who you are. You are a ray of God's own light.'

'Sounds a bit silly,' the young man thought to himself. But he was intrigued, so he said, 'What do you mean?'

'You say you seek God, but a ray of light doesn't seek the sun; it's coming from the sun. You are a branch on the vine of God. A branch doesn't seek the vine; it's already part of the vine. A wave doesn't look for the ocean; it's already full of ocean. Because you don't know that who you are is one with God, you believe all these labels about yourself: I'm a sinner, I'm a saint, I'm a wretch, I'm a worm and no man, I'm a monk, I'm a nurse. These are all labels, clothing. They serve a purpose, but they are not who you are. To the extent that you believe these labels, you believe a lie, and you add anguish upon anguish. It's what most of us do for most of our lives. In the secular world we call it our career. In monastic terms, we call it our vocation.'

'Before you can know in your own experience what the Psalmist meant when he said, "Be still and know that I am God," you must first learn to be still and know who you are. The rest will follow.'

Then Fr Alypius said, 'Tell me about your prayer.'

'Well, I never miss the community prayers,' the young man replied.

'I didn't ask you about saying your prayers. I asked about *prayer.*'

'Do you mean silent prayer?'

'Tell me about that.'

'I have trouble being silent,' said the young man.

'But you already are silent. I understand how there is a lot of noise and chaos swirling around. That's true of us all. But you, you are silence. You are the silence that is aware of the chaos. You are the silence that sees the chaos. Again, I tell you, you don't know who you are.'

'What's all this chaos, then?' asked the young man.

'It's just weather. Tell me, what happens when you sit in silence?'

'I try to give myself over to contemplation and then get lost in thoughts.'

'But silence,' Fr Alypius said, 'silence and contemplation are concerned with what is deeper than thinking, with that vastness in which the things going on in your head appear. When this vastness full of vibrant emptiness is recognized to be the centre of all appearances, even the inner chaos, then it becomes obvious that contemplation, silence, is always present.'

'I think I've glimpsed something of this, but normally I'm just lost in my thoughts,' confessed the young man.

'Are you? I thought you were a ray of God's own light, a branch on the vine. Now you say you are something different. You say you are someone lost in thoughts. But isn't this thought, "I am lost in my thoughts," just another thought, just another label that is being believed? We assume we are our thoughts, but look and see. Are you lost in your thoughts?'

'Not right now. But if I went back and tried to sit in silence, there would just be this inner chatter. I know my mind should be quiet. I should be having no thoughts.'

Fr Alypius continued his instruction. 'These new thoughts: "my mind should be quiet"; "I shouldn't be having thoughts," are noisier than the previous thoughts. But these particular thoughts are believed to be the truth. Believing them to be the truth distracts you from the deeper reality. Silence is naturally present. Silence cannot not be there. When you think, "I'm lost in my thoughts; my mind should be silent," just stop for a second and ask: "*Who* is lost? *Who* is not quiet?" Do it right now.'

There was a pause. The young man looked hard.

Fr Alypius asked him, 'When you look directly into the thought, do you see someone who is lost?'

'No, there is no one there. There is no one who is lost. In that moment there is not a chatterer, but then that moment is gone and all the chatter comes back.'

'That's right,' cheered Fr Alypius. 'Thoughts keep coming back because that's just what thoughts do. But if you look directly at the thought or feeling and ask who is the chatterer, who is suffering, you won't find anybody, you won't find a sufferer. There will be chattering, sure. Suffering, sure. The thoughts coming and going. Don't look at the suffering, the anguish, the fear. These are objects of awareness. I'm asking you to look into the awareness itself. Not the objects of awareness. These have dominated your attention for decades. Let your attention rest in the awareness, not the objects of awareness. Yes, I can see on your face. The mind grows still. Tell me what do you see?'

'Nothing,' said the young man. 'Just this vast nothing.'

'Tell me, what is the substance of all this chatter and chaos in your head?'

The young man responded, 'It's just fluff.'

'That's right,' said Fr Alypius. 'Do you see how simple it is? It is not special or rarefied. It's not because you've been chanting for nine hours straight or fasting for the last three weeks.

These monastic strategies are of no use because it has already been accomplished. When you see that you are caught up in the storms of chaos, inner chatter, and mental commentary, ask yourself, "Who am I?" Ask "*Who* is experiencing the chaos? *Who* is chattering? *Who* is the commentator?" You won't find anyone there checking to see if you are caught in thoughts. When you turn your attention from the object of your awareness to the awareness itself, there is just silent, vast, openness that has never been wounded, harmed, angry, frightened, incomplete. This is who you are.'

On many evenings the young man would make his way down to the bottom of the garden for conversations with Fr Alypius. They were all about the question, 'Who am I?' The young man grew in wisdom and in this paradox of identity, and there was a great calm about him. On their final meeting Fr Alypius said, 'You have mastered the question, "Who am I?" I would like to put to you another question: "Who is Jesus Christ?"' The young man was fixed in a silent, inner gaze. As he looked at the young man, Fr Alypius's face brightened; he could see that the young man knew. He sat back and returned to repairing a shoe and said to the young man, 'Well done. Now off with you. I believe the abbot wants to have a word with you.'

Guided visualization: growing up in a gay world[2]

I'd like you to imagine being adopted by a gay couple as a baby. Suspend any judgements or questions about how and why. Imagine your feelings if your primary caregivers were either two lesbians or two gay men. Pick one or the other couple and get in touch with your feelings.

These people love you very much and are proud of you. You love them too and want them to be proud. These men or women looked after you when you were sick, walked you to your first day of school, taught you to read, bought you your first bicycle. What would that be like?

What would it be like if these gay people had other children too – children who identified themselves as gay? Your older brother has a boyfriend he holds hands with. You have seen your older sister kissing her girlfriend. What would that feel like?

And what would it feel like if all the others thought you were gay too? Not only do they think you are gay, they expect you to be gay. In a variety of ways, they let you know that if you want to make them proud, if you want to make them happy, if you want to be always welcomed, you will one day bring home someone of the same sex. They are counting on you being gay. How do you feel – and who do you tell how you feel?

Imagine another scenario. You are 14 years old and on your way to school. You sit next to your friend on the bus. Without figuring out how and why it would work, how would it feel to be 14 years old, sitting next to your best friend who is gay, and who thinks you are too, singing a gay song the gay bus driver has turned up on the gay radio station? How would it feel if every song you ever heard was written by one gay person to another? What if every book you read, every film you saw, every advert you passed in the street featured the beauty and joy of gay love? How do you feel – and who do you tell how you feel?

Now, not everyone is a happy, healthy homosexual. There are people who are thought to be sexually obsessed with people of the other sex. No one ever talks about them, unless it's to make a joke, but you've heard about them: these people are technically called heterosexuals, but most people refer to them as breeders. Even though the breeders have, in recent years, managed to get some laws passed to give them some protection and political rights, there are still many people who think they are sick; it's still OK for religious groups to express prejudice and hatred towards breeders – you heard someone on the radio recently talking about how they believed that all breeders would go to hell because of their sexual behaviour.

At school, someone wrote on the toilet wall 'Kelly is a breeder' and no one sat with Kelly all week. The boy suspected of being a breeder was teased all the time and was always the last one to get picked for team sports. The girl suspected of being a breeder had her locker trashed on a regular basis. How do you feel – and who would you tell how you feel?

Your teacher is gay. The head of school is gay. The school counsellor is gay. Everyone thinks you are too.

Back home, the phone rings and you are called to speak to Chris. Chris – who is the same sex as you – wants to take you to the school's first dance of the year on Friday. Even though you somehow feel uncomfortable about going along, you know that this is what you're supposed to do. So you say yes. At school, everyone seems excited about this dance, but you don't – it feels somehow scary and difficult, but you're not sure why. Why don't you enjoy going out with people and having a good time? You don't know why – but you often feel uncomfortable in these situations.

At the dance, the hall is filled with same-sex couples. Initially, it is not too bad because the music is fast. But now it's slow. Slow dance after slow dance has you in Chris's arms. He or she is holding you tight, nuzzling your neck, whispering in your ear: 'Are you having fun?'

Every day it's the same. To be popular you'd better have a steady boyfriend if you're a man, or a steady girlfriend if you're a woman. Pass the love notes in class; put their name in a big heart on your notebook; go out on dates to gay films and gay parties; kiss them, tell them you love them. But what do you feel – and who do you talk to?

Sometimes, when you're watching films you find yourself more attracted to members of the opposite sex than the same sex, but you feel ashamed of this and try not to think about it. When a breeder comes on TV your parents always make sarcastic comments, and say things like 'That's disgusting' – you know that it's wrong to have feelings like this and you try really hard not to think about them. Maybe this is just a phase you're going through. Do you think there might be a book about being a breeder in the school library? And if there is, do you have the courage to take it off the shelf, hand it to the gay librarian, and risk someone seeing you with it? You wonder whether the school counsellor might help you to understand but you know that they have a same-sex partner too so they probably won't be much help.

You start to feel really confused by your feelings – and wonder if they'll change in time so that you can fit in with everyone else and feel normal. You start to get a bit withdrawn and to avoid going out; sometimes it seems that people around you are learning how to live, and you are learning how to hide. Your parents start asking when you're going to bring someone nice home for them to meet – and this makes you feel a bit panicky; you don't know what to say, or how to respond. You just know that it makes you feel really anxious. You'd love to talk to your parents about how you're feeling – but you also know that they'd be really upset if you told them about what's going on for you. Especially one of them, who is quite breeder-phobic, and who often says how disgusting it is that there are so many of them now in public life. 'Why can't they keep quiet about it all – I don't go round telling everyone that I'm gay,' they say.

As the years go by, your attraction for the opposite sex grows, but you still haven't really told anyone about it. Your elder sister is really breeder-phobic and often goes on about how much she hates them and how disgusting they are. Your younger brother is too young to talk to and anyway, you're not sure he'd really understand. How do you feel – and who do you tell how you feel?

When you're 18 it's time to leave home and go to university. You're really looking forward to it because you heard that there is a society there for people like you who are more attracted to the opposite sex. You're hoping that meeting other people like you might help you to feel better about yourself and understand why you feel like this. But you hadn't fully realized what it would be like living in a flat with other gay people, some of whom are quite aggressive about breeders – it's quite intimidating being around them all the time, especially when they are always asking you about your relationships, and who you like the look of. Some of them get drunk a lot, and then things get very awkward because some of them start saying things like, 'You're a breeder, aren't you?' One night, a group of them stood outside your door shouting, 'Come out, breeder, we know you're in there.' When you are in your room alone, how do you feel – and who do you tell how you feel?

You make it along to the first meeting of the breeders society, feeling very nervous – and unfortunately it doesn't go very well. The people there seem so confident! They are really loud and in your face – it's hard to tell them how nervous you feel or how uncertain you are about everything. Some of them seem quite nice, but at the end of the evening, you're quite glad to just get back to your room and shut the door. It feels safer there – even if you do get quite lonely at times. Sometimes you log on to some websites where you can chat to other people who are attracted to the opposite sex and it's quite interesting but you wonder if you really want to be like them: their lives seem so sad and empty. All they seem to be interested in is sex. And a lot of them say that they'd rather be gay – it'd be just so much easier. That's when you start to feel quite depressed and desperate – but who do you tell about how you're feeling? You thought that coming away to university would be more fun than this – that you'd meet lots of people who are like you – but somehow it isn't working out like that.

One person you'd love to talk to, one of your parents, is the last person you feel you can approach. You haven't told any of your flatmates that you're straight and going along to straight-soc always leaves you feeling alienated and more alone than before. Surely there must be someone who can understand and help you think about how to cope?

You're 18 – you think you might be straight – you wish you weren't – you haven't told your parents – and you haven't really come out to many people your own age: after 18 years of feeling different, of feeling like an outsider, how do you feel – and who do you tell how you feel?

Notes

1 Hearing the call

1 It should be noted that elsewhere in the Bible, God does call people from wholly outside Israel, such as the Persian king Cyrus.

2 Understanding the call

1 Matthew Kelty, in *Thomas Merton, Monk: A Monastic Tribute*, ed. Patrick Hart, London: Hodder and Stoughton, 1975, p. 27.

3 Surely it's not me?

1 J. Palmer Parker, *Let Your Life Speak*, San Francisco: John Wiley, 2000, pp. 10, 25.
2 Thomas Merton, *Seeds of Contemplation*, Wheathampstead: Anthony Clarke, 1961, p. 25.
3 Merton, *Seeds of Contemplation*, p. 125.
4 U. A. Fanthorpe, *Collected Poems 1978–2003*, Cornwall: Peterloo Poets, 2005, pp. 108–9. Reproduced by permission.
5 Quoted in Esther De Waal, *A Seven Day Journey with Thomas Merton*, Guildford: Eagle, 2000, p. 44.
6 D. Linn, S. F. Linn and M. Linn, *Sleeping with Bread*, Mahwah, NJ: Paulist Press, 1995.
7 Summer Congregation for Durham University, 2012. © Professor Simon Hackett, Durham University. Reproduced by permission.
8 Augustine, *On Christian Doctrine* IV, 27:59.
9 Walter Brueggemann, *A Commentary on Jeremiah: Exile and Home-coming*, Grand Rapids, MI: Eerdmans, 1998, p. 202.

4 The foolishness of God's call

1 Adrian Plass, *Clearing Away the Rubbish*, Eastbourne: Kingsway Publications, 1988, pp. 175–7. Reproduced by permission.
2 Quoted in Michael Mayne, *A Year Lost and Found*, London: Darton, Longman and Todd, 1987, p. 70.
3 A good introduction to this ministry can be found in L. Roger Owens, *Abba, Give Me A Word*, Brewster, MA: Paraclete Press, 2012.

4 Thomas Merton, *Thoughts in Solitude*, 3rd edn, London and New York: Burns and Oates, 1997, p. 81.
5 Dag Hammarskjöld, *Markings*, London: Faber and Faber, 1964, p. 87.
6 Richard North, *Fools for God*, London: Collins, 1987.
7 Thomas Merton, quoted in Angela Ashwin, *Faith in the Fool*, London: Darton, Longman and Todd: 2009, p. 66.
8 Roly Bain, quoted in Ashwin, *Faith in the Fool*, p. 19.
9 Eugene Peterson, *Under the Unpredictable Plant*, Chicago: Eerdmans, 1992, pp. 140–2.

5 The counter-cultural nature of call

1 William Golding, *The Spire*, London: Faber and Faber, 1964, p. 121.
2 Quoted in Peter Lomas, *True and False Experience*, London: Transaction Publishers, 1994, pp. 94–5. Copyright © 1994 by Transaction Publishers. Reprinted by permission of the publisher.
3 Quoted by Terry Eagleton in *London Review of Books*, Vol. 28 No. 20, 19 October 2006, pp. 32–4.
4 J. K. Galbraith, *The Nature of Mass Poverty*, 1979, quoted in Philippe Legrain, *Immigrants: Your Country Needs Them*, London: Little, Brown, 2006, p. 1.
5 All the italics in this chapter are mine.

6 The subversive nature of God's call

1 William Barry, *Paying Attention to God*, Notre Dame, IN: Ave Maria Press, 2004.
2 J. C. Fenton, *St Matthew*, Harmondsworth: Penguin, 1963: p. 42.
3 London: Darton, Longman and Todd, 1978, p. 93.
4 Quoted in *Watch for the Light*, Farmington, PA: Plough Publishing House, 2001; entry for 30 November.
5 Maria Boulding, *The Coming of God*, London: SPCK, 1982, p. 25.
6 Evelyn Underhill, *Concerning the Inner Life*, Oxford: Oneworld Publications, 2000.
7 Underhill, *Concerning the Inner Life*, p. 18.

7 God's call and failure

1 Eugene Peterson, *Subversive Spirituality*, Grand Rapids, MI: Eerdmans, 1997, p. 12.
2 Peterson, *Subversive Spirituality*, p. 237.

3 John Sanford, *Ministry Burnout*, Louisville, KY: Westminster, 1982, p. 6.
4 Mark Townsend, *The Gospel of Falling Down*, Winchester: O Books, 2007; Vanessa Herrick and Ivan Mann, *Jesus Wept*, London: Darton, Longman and Todd, 1998.
5 Jean Vanier, *Community and Growth*, London: Darton, Longman and Todd, 1989, p. 96.
6 There is a trailer on YouTube: < www.youtube.com/watch?v=rfLxYnTg2zI>.
7 Quoted in Townsend, *The Gospel of Falling Down*, pp. 51–2.
8 Quoted in Urs Mattman, *Coming In*, Glasgow: Wild Goose Publications, 2006, p. 11.
9 Quoted in Townsend, *The Gospel of Falling Down*, p. 53.
10 Carol Carretto, *Letters From the Desert*, London: Darton, Longman and Todd, 1990, pp. 14–16.
11 Quoted in Wanda Nash, *Come Let Us Play!*, London: Darton, Longman and Todd, 1999, p. 69.
12 Evelyn Underhill, *Worship*, London: Nisbet and Co., 1937, p. 17.
13 Peterson, *Subversive Spirituality*, p. 76.

8 'Let anyone who has an ear listen to what the Spirit is saying to the churches'

1 Ann Belford Ulanov, *The Wizards' Gate*, Switzerland: Daimon, 1994, p. 28.
2 James Hollis, *The Middle Passage*, Toronto: Inner City Books, 1993, p. 72.
3 Jean Vanier, *Growth and Community*, London: Darton, Longman and Todd, 1989, p. 124.
4 Gerard W. Hughes, *God of Surprises*, London: Darton, Longman and Todd, 1985, pp. 104–11.
5 Owen Chadwick, *Michael Ramsey*, Oxford: Oxford University Press, 1990, p. 398.
6 Thomas Merton, *The Silent Life*, London: Burns and Oates, 1957, p. 41.

Endnote

1 Martin Laird, *Into the Silent Land*, London: Darton, Longman and Todd, 2006, pp. 133–42. Reproduced by permission.
2 Based on an original idea by Chuck Stewart in *Sexually Stigmatized Communities: Reducing Heterosexism and Homophobia – An Awareness Training Manual*, Thousand Oaks, CA: Sage Publications, 1999.